Super Science

HighReach Learning®, Inc. is committed to creating high-quality, developmentally appropriate learning materials that facilitate a creative, integrated, hands-on learning experience for the whole child. Our goal is to enhance the development of readiness skills and encourage a love for learning in every young child.

Author: Beverly A. Warkulwiz
Editor: Tammy A. Willis
Copy Editor: Barbara C. Kirchner, Pamela R. Jarrell
Design and Layout: Nancy Rentschler
Illustrator: Deborah C. Johnson

Printed in the USA. All rights reserved.   ISBN 978-1-57332-466-3

Table of contents

Introduction

Young children are naturally curious. By simply building upon this innate curiosity, you can make science come alive! Although teaching science may seem daunting at first, it can be an enjoyable experience for both you and the children.

Why is teaching science to young children important?

As adults, we frequently take a scientific approach to problem solving in our daily lives, but learning how to think scientifically develops over a lifetime. By encouraging children to utilize scientific thinking skills (questioning, predicting, reasoning, experimenting, and applying what is learned), children begin to build a foundation for lifelong learning.

Where do I begin?

It important to thoughtfully plan authentic experiences that are interesting and meaningful to children. It is equally important to remain flexible enough to build upon the children's impromptu discoveries about the natural world and how it works.

Approach teaching science as a frame of mind:
- Establish an environment where asking questions is not only accepted, but encouraged.
- Facilitate explorations through guided inquiry – asking leading questions and guiding children to construct their own knowledge (rather than providing answers).
- Invite the children to make predictions and share what they have learned.
- Provide numerous opportunities for hands-on and "minds-on" experiences.
- Encourage the children to have fun... and the learning will fall into place!

How should I structure my science lessons?

Much of your science teaching should evolve from informal conversations with the children. Look for "teachable moments" in every situation. As the children discover something new, take time to explore it further together. Scientific skills can be integrated into just about every experience. Building with blocks, playing with sand, pouring drinks at snack time, tossing a ball into the air, observing shadows on a sunny day, or even finger painting can all become scientific moments.

Science experiences and other related activities are most effective when working with small groups of children. Within a small group setting, children have a greater number of opportunities to become actively engaged in learning. At the beginning of each experience, invite the children to share what they already know (or think they know) about what you are studying. You may want to record their thoughts on chart paper along with questions they have about the concept. During the activity, encourage the children to interact with each other and the materials. At the end of each experience, invite the children to share what they have learned.

What if I don't know the answer?

Undoubtedly, a child will ask a question that you cannot answer. When this happens, explore the question together. Remember, it is more important for young children to be engaged in thinking scientifically than it is for them to have all the answers. What a wonderful opportunity to show the children that learning is something you do throughout your entire life!

> "Learning science is an active process... something students do, not something that is done to them."
> (*National Science Education Standards, 1996*)

How to use this book

Asking questions is the basis of all scientific exploration. Since science is rooted in inquiry, each topic in this book begins with an essential question. As you glance through the book, you will notice a wide variety of activities integrating science with music, art, dramatic play, math, language, and more! Through these hands-on and "minds-on" activities, scientific process skills (see chart below) are woven into the exploration of each essential question. In addition, you will find a comprehensive list of children's literature that can be used to further extend each science concept (pp. 6-7).

This book has been designed for use in two possible ways:
- To explore in sequence – The essential questions and their activities are listed in a logical order so one question/activity builds upon the next.
- To extend and enhance your existing curriculum – Choose activities which are applicable to your science curriculum.

Note: No matter how you utilize the resource, choose activities that best meet the readiness levels and interests of the children.

As you begin to plan, use the essential questions at the top of each page and the activity icons to help you:

 Building Bridges *(connecting prior knowledge with new knowledge)*

 Tune Time *(songs and rhythmic activities)*

 Large Muscle Skills *(and other interpersonal activities)*

 Language Activities

 Fine Motor Skills

 Scientific Explorations

 Let's Pretend!

 Mathematical Thinking

 Art Experiences

Assume the role of facilitator and guide:
The scientific information in this book is primarily intended for the teacher's use. However, as the children explore each concept, you can help them discover much of the information on their own. Remember that the teacher's role in the "science classroom" should be facilitator and guide, not dispenser of information.

One final thought before you embark on your scientific adventure...
If you show enthusiasm for science, the children will too. Your excitement will surely affect how the children feel about science for years to come. Introduce young children to the world of science – and you will nurture a love of learning that will last a lifetime!

Process Skills:
- Wonder
- Ask questions
- Hypothesize
- Predict
- Estimate
- Observe
- Record
- Describe
- Experiment
- Measure
- Analyze
- Reason
- Conclude
- Discuss
- Apply

Literature connections

Enhance literacy development by sharing books that correspond with the science concepts found in *Super Science*. Below you will find a comprehensive list of both nonfiction and realistic fiction. Use these books to further explore each concept through words and/or pictures. If the following titles are unavailable, consult a librarian for alternate suggestions.

My Five Senses

- *My Five Senses/Mis cinco sentidos* by Aliki
- *My Five Senses* by Margaret Miller
- *You Can't Smell a Flower With Your Ear! All About Your 5 Senses* by Beverly Collins

Plants

- *What's Alive?* by Kathleen Weidner Zoehfeld
- *From Seed to Plant* by Gail Gibbons
- *How a Seed Grows/Cómo crece una semilla* by Helene J. Jordan
- *Carrot Seed* by Ruth Krauss
- *Pumpkin Pumpkin* by Jeanne Titherington
- *One Child, One Seed: A South African Counting Book* by Kathryn Cave
- *The Tiny Seed* by Eric Carle
- *Planting a Rainbow/Cómo plantar un arco iris* by Lois Ehlert
- *Jack's Garden* by Henry Cole
- *Flower Garden* by Eve Bunting

Animals – Farm and Zoo

- *Farm Animals* by DK Publishing
- *Big Red Barn/El gran granero rojo* by Margaret Wise Brown
- *My Visit to the Zoo* by Aliki
- *Polar Bear, Polar Bear, What Do You Hear?/Oso polar, oso polar, ¿qué es ese ruido?* by Bill Martin Jr.

Animals – Habitats

- *I See a Kookaburra! Discovering Animal Habitats Around the World* by Steve Jenkins & Robin Page
- *In the Small, Small Pond* by Denise Fleming
- *Life in a Forest* by Carol K. Lindeen
- *Slowly, Slowly, Slowly, Said the Sloth* by Eric Carle
- *North Pole, South Pole* by Nancy Smiler Levinson
- *Ocean* by Samantha Gray
- *Here Is the African Savanna* by Madeleine Dunphy
- *Way Out in the Desert* by T.J. Marsh and Jennifer Ward

Animals – Types of

- *About Mammals: A Guide for Children* by Cathryn P. Sill
- *Animals Born Alive and Well* by Ruth Heller
- *Water Beds: Sleeping in the Ocean* by Gail Langer Karwoski
- *About Birds: A Guide for Children* by Cathryn P. Sill
- *Puffins Climb, Penguins Rhyme* by Bruce McMillan
- *Fish Eyes: A Book You Can Count On* by Lois Ehlert
- *Little Shark* by Anne Rockwell
- *I Am a Little Alligator* by Francois Crozat
- *Turtles* by Jodi Huelin
- *Frogs* by Gail Gibbons
- *From Tadpole to Frog* by Wendy Pfeffer
- *Red-eyed Tree Frog* by Joy Cowley
- *Jump, Frog, Jump!/¡Salta, ranita, salta!* by Robert Kalan
- *San Diego Zoo Animal Library* by Ideals Publications
- *Baby Animals Learn* by Pamela Chanko
- *Is Your Mama a Llama?/¿Tu mamá es una llama?* by Deborah Guarino
- *Starfish* by Edith Thacher Hurd
- *An Octopus Is Amazing* by Patricia Lauber
- *A House for Hermit Crab* by Eric Carle

Literature connections

- *Mister Seahorse* by Eric Carle
- *What Do Insects Do?* by Susan Canizares
- *The Very Quiet Cricket* by Eric Carle
- *From Caterpillar to Butterfly* by Deborah Heiligman
- *Are You a Butterfly?* by Judy Allen
- *Spiders* by Gail Gibbons
- *Diary of a Spider* by Doreen Cronin
- *Diary of a Worm* by Doreen Cronin
- *Wonderful Worms* by Linda Glaser

Animals – Extinct & Endangered

- *Mammals of Long Ago* by Allan Fowler
- *Endangered Animals* by Faith McNulty
- *Panda Bear, Panda Bear, What Do You See?* by Bill Martin Jr.
- *The Great Kapok Tree: A Tale of the Amazon Rain Forest/El gran capoquero: Un cuento de la selva amazonica* by Lynne Cherry
- *The Eyes of Gray Wolf* by Jonathan London
- *Uno's Garden* by Graeme Base

Animals – Fossils & Dinosaurs

- *Fossils Tell of Long Ago/Los fósiles hablan nos del pasado* by Aliki
- *Dinosaurs* by Gail Gibbons
- *How Big Were the Dinosaurs?* by Bernard Most
- *What Happened to the Dinosaurs?* by Franklyn M. Branley
- *Dinosaur Roar!* by Paul and Henrietta Stickland

Earth & Space – Water, Weather, & Land

- *The Earth Is Mostly Ocean* by Allan Fowler
- *The Seven Continents* by Wil Mara
- *I Love Our Earth* by Bill Martin Jr. and Michael Sampson
- *Our Big Home: An Earth Poem* by Linda Glaser

- *Water Dance* by Thomas Locker
- *Cloud Dance* by Thomas Locker
- *The Cloud Book/El libro de las nubes* by Tomie dePaola
- *A Drop Around the World* by Barbara Shaw McKinney
- *The Water Cycle* by Don Curry
- *Down Comes the Rain* by Franklyn M. Branley
- *Snow is Falling* by Franklyn M. Branley
- *The Snowflake: A Water Cycle Story* by Neil Waldman
- *White Snow, Bright Snow* by Alvin Tresselt
- *Everybody Needs a Rock* by Byrd Baylor
- *In the Dark Cave* by Richard A. Watson

Earth & Space – Save the Earth

- *Pollution* by Janine Amos
- *Oil Spill!* by Melvin Berger
- *The Wump World* by Bill Peet
- *The Berenstain Bears Don't Pollute (Anymore)* by Stan and Jan Berenstain
- *The Great Trash Bash* by Loreen Leedy
- *Where Does the Garbage Go?* by Paul Showers
- *Why Should I Recycle?* by Jen Green
- *Why Should I Save Water?* by Jen Green

Earth & Space – Space

- *Space* by Simon Holland
- *The Sun: Our Nearest Star* by Franklyn M. Branley
- *When You Look Up at the Moon* by Allan Fowler

Exploration Station

- *All the Colors of the Rainbow* by Allan Fowler
- *Shadows and Reflections* by Tana Hoban
- *Moonbear's Shadow* by Frank Asch
- *Air Is All Around You* by Franklyn M. Branley
- *Bubble Bubble* by Mercer Mayer
- *Will It Float or Sink?* by Melissa Stewart
- *What Magnets Can Do* by Allan Fowler

Scientists use their senses to learn more about the world around them. As you begin to establish an atmosphere of scientific exploration in your classroom, you may want to start with the basics – the five senses.

My 5 Senses

What are my five senses?

Building Bridges: The Five Senses

Like scientists, we use our five senses every day. Share the rhyme below with the children and encourage them to join in. After reciting the rhyme a few times, invite the children to make observations of their surroundings "like scientists."

My Five Senses

I have two eyes to help me see.
I have two ears to help me hear.
I have a nose to help me smell.
I have a tongue to help me taste.
I have two hands to help me touch.
My senses help me very much!

Point to your eyes.
Point to your ears.
Point to your nose.
Point to your mouth.
Show your hands.

Popping Popcorn – A "Sense-ational" Experience

Encourage the children to explore popcorn using their senses. Of course, no popcorn experience would be complete without tasting it in the end!

- Give each child a few kernels of unpopped popcorn in a disposable cup. What do the kernels look like? How do they sound when you shake them in the cup? What do they feel like?
- Pop some popcorn using an air popper. Have the children describe what they see, hear, and smell.
- Give each child a sample of popped popcorn. Does it look and feel the same as before? How is it different?
- After the children are done exploring, invite them to enjoy this "sense-ational" snack.

Caution: To prevent choking, do not allow the children to eat the kernels.

Variation: Explore pumpkins using your five senses. What does a pumpkin look like (outside and inside)? When you knock on a pumpkin, does it make a sound? What does the inside of a pumpkin smell like? What does a pumpkin feel like (outside and inside)? Finally, try samples of pumpkin treats (e.g., bread, pie, baked seeds) and have the children describe how they taste. Yummy!

People who have lost their sense of sight or hearing face many challenges. Completing daily tasks, carrying on conversations, even participating in favorite pastimes can all prove to be very challenging. However, blind or deaf people often find that their other senses are heightened, compensating for the loss of their sight or hearing.

Building Bridges: Describe What You See

We use our eyes to learn more about the world around us. Our eyes help us determine color, shape, size, and other distinguishable features. Encourage the children to look around the classroom and/or playground area and describe what they see.

Explore Shapes and Colors

Set out pattern blocks, shape stickers, and/or several shapes cut from various colors of cardstock. Invite the children to explore the shapes and colors by sorting, forming patterns, or using the shapes to create designs. As the children are working, encourage them to name the shapes and colors.

Monet, DaVinci, Picasso, and Me!

Show the children a few paintings by well-known artists, such as Monet, DaVinci, or Picasso, and have the children describe what they see. Invite the children to express their creativity by painting their very own masterpieces.

Play What's Missing?

Challenge the children to use their eyes (and their brains) to try to identify the missing objects in the following game. Place some familiar objects on a table. Encourage the children to look carefully at the objects, and then close their eyes. Remove one object and place it out of the children's sight. Have the children try to determine which object is missing. Before you replace the object, challenge the children to describe it. Repeat the game, each time removing a different object.

> **Variation:** Choose one child to be the Detective. Allow the Detective time to observe all the children, then have the Detective turn around and close his/her eyes. Tap one child on the shoulder and have him/her hide. Invite the Detective to turn back around and try to determine who is missing. Repeat the game, each time choosing a different Detective and child who will hide.

I Use My Eyes to See

(tune: "The Farmer in the Dell")

I use my eyes to see.
I use my eyes to see –
To see the world around me.
I use my eyes to see.

What can I do with my ears?

Building Bridges: Everyday Sounds

Make a tape of everyday sounds (e.g., birds chirping, wind blowing, car beeping, phone ringing, toilet flushing). As you play the tape, invite the children to guess what the sounds could be.

Variations:
(1) Record each child in the class saying, "Hello! Can you guess who I am?" Play the tape and encourage the children to match the voices to their classroom friends.
(2) Put small everyday objects in margarine tubs with lids (one item in each tub). Place a set of matching objects on the table. Encourage the children to shake the containers and try to determine which item is in each tub.

Repeat the Beat

Experimenting with music and rhythm is an easy and fun way to learn more about sound. Clap various sound patterns and have the children repeat after you. (See examples listed below.) As the children demonstrate success, challenge them by making the patterns more complicated or including other sounds/motions, such as stomping or tapping hands on thighs. Invite the children to share their own sound patterns with the class, as well.

Examples of sound patterns:
- clap clap
- clap stomp
- clap clap stomp clap

Decorate and Play Drums

Preparation:
◊ Collect several oatmeal containers with lids.
◊ Set out the containers and a variety of art materials.

Invite the children to decorate the containers to make drums. Play recorded music in the background, and encourage the children to beat their drums in time with the music.

I Use My Ears to Hear
(tune: "The Farmer in the Dell")

I use my ears to hear.
I use my ears to hear –
Laugh out loud and give a cheer.
I use my ears to hear.

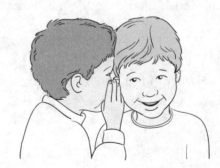

What can I do with my nose?

Building Bridges: Good Smells, Bad Smells

Preparation:
◊ Draw two columns on chart paper.
◊ Print "Good Smells" on the top left with a happy face.
◊ Print "Bad Smells" on the top right with a yucky face.

Ask the children to name some good smells (e.g., flowers) and bad smells (e.g., trash), and list their examples on the chart in the appropriate columns. Encourage the children to share stories about how different smells remind them of certain things, places, or experiences. For example, "The smell of popcorn reminds me of the movies," or "When I smell a skunk, I remember camping with my family." After the children have shared their "smelly" stories, invite them to create pictures about their experiences.

Good Smells	Bad Smells
😊	😖
Flowers	Trash

Match the Scents

Preparation:
◊ Place scented items or liquid extracts in disposable cups. Prepare two cups for each scent. Be sure to use distinctly different scents (e.g., vinegar, coffee, cinnamon, vanilla, mint).
◊ Cover the cups with foil and tape around the sides.
◊ Make a few smalls holes in the foil to allow the scents to escape.

Invite the children to smell each cup and try to find another cup with the same scent. As the children explore, ask engaging questions such as: What does that scent remind you of? Which scent do you like the most? Which do you like the least? Why?

Explore Scented Playdough

Add a package of orange powdered drink mix to orange playdough and a package of strawberry powdered drink mix to red playdough. Set out the playdough, assorted cookie cutters, and toy rolling pins. Invite the children to explore the playdough and talk about the scents that they smell.

I Use My Nose to Smell

(tune: "The Farmer in the Dell")

I use my nose to smell.
I use my nose to smell –
I smell scents so very well.
I use my nose to smell.

Super Science

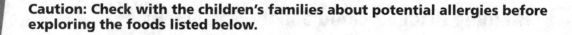

What can I do with my tongue?

Caution: Check with the children's families about potential allergies before exploring the foods listed below.

Building Bridges: "Tasty" Foods

Invite the children to try foods with different tastes. For example, pudding is sweet, lemons are sour, pretzels are salty, and unsweetened baking cocoa is bitter. Introduce the words sweet, *sour*, *salty*, and *bitter* as the children taste the foods.

Taste and Graph Foods

Preparation:
- ◊ Draw four columns on chart paper to make a graph.
- ◊ Attach a picture of each food the children will taste across the bottom of the graph. Put one picture in each column.
- ◊ Prepare samples of foods for the children to taste.

Invite the children to try foods with different tastes. Give each child a sticker and invite the children to place the stickers above their favorite foods from the taste test. Count the stickers to discover which food is liked the best and which is liked the least.

Note: You may want to combine this activity with the "Tasty" Foods activity (see above).

Try a Tasty Trick

Preparation:
- ◊ Dip cotton balls in vanilla extract and set aside to dry.
- ◊ Cut apple slices and place the knife out of the children's reach.

Did you know that your senses of smell and taste are connected? Your sense of smell affects how you perceive what you taste. Invite the children to trick their taste buds by following these steps:

- ☿ Take a bite of the apple and notice how it tastes.
- ☿ Hold a cotton ball near your nose and smell it.
- ☿ Take another bite of the apple while still smelling the cotton ball.
- ☿ The apple should taste like vanilla!

I Use My Tongue to Taste

(tune: "The Farmer in the Dell")

I use my tongue to taste.
I use my tongue to taste –
Bitter, salty, sweet, and sour.
I use my tongue to taste.

What can I do with my hands?

Building Bridges: Explore Textures

Set out items with distinctly different textures, such as feathers, felt, sandpaper, cotton balls, foil, hook and loop tape, and silk scarves. As the children explore the materials with their sense of touch, ask questions about the different textures (e.g., Is it smooth or rough? Is it silky or scratchy?).

Variation: Invite each child to trace one hand on construction paper, cut it out, and glue textured materials onto the cutouts.

Mystery Boxes

Preparation:
◊ Collect several shoe boxes with lids.
◊ Cut a hole in the side of each box large enough to reach inside.
◊ Choose a variety of objects with distinctly different textures and place one item in each box.

Invite the children to reach inside the boxes and try to identify the objects. Reveal the objects after the children have had an opportunity to explore all of the boxes.

Make Goop

Give each child a disposable bowl, ¼ cup cornstarch, and about 3 tablespoons of water. Talk about what the cornstarch feels like before adding water. Have the children add water to the cornstarch little by little and mix it with their hands. If the mixture seems too dry, add a few more drops of water until it reaches the desired consistency (can roll into a ball, but flows like liquid in palm of hand). Invite the children to use their sense of touch to explore the goop.

I Use My Hands to Touch
(tune: "The Farmer in the Dell")

I use my hands to touch.
I use my hands to touch –
My hands help me very much.
I use my hands to touch.

The next time that you're outside, look around you. What do you see? From the tallest tree to the tiniest blade of grass – plants are everywhere! So many questions come to mind as one begins to explore living things. Through the following activities, children will have several hands-on opportunities to learn about plants and begin to discover the answers to some of their questions.

Caution: Before doing any of the outdoor activities in this section, check with the children's families about allergies to plants and animals that might be encountered outside.

Plants

Are plants living things?
What do living things need to live?

Building Bridges: Living and Nonliving Things

Preparation:

◊ Draw or cut out pictures of living and nonliving things (e.g., plants, animals, rocks, classroom objects, toys).
◊ Attach each picture to a separate index card.

Invite the children to sort the cards, but do not tell the how the pictures should be sorted at first. After exploring a few ideas, ask the children to sort the cards into two groups – things that are living (alive) and things that are not. After the children have sorted the cards, explain that plants and other living things need water, food, and air to live.

Variation: Challenge the children to further sort the pictures of living things into plants and animals. Explain that the main difference between plants and animals is that plants make their own food whereas animals need to eat.

Living Things

(tune: chorus of "Jingle Bells")

Living things, living things
Need water, food, and air.
Plants and animals are alive,
But not my teddy bear.

Living things, living things
They all change and grow.
Birds and bees, and flowers and trees,
And the grass we mow!

Create Collages

Invite the children to tear or cut pictures of living things from magazines and glue the pictures onto construction paper. As the children are working, talk about what living things need.

Pet Rocks

Set out a variety of art materials and several smooth rocks. Invite the children to make "pets" using the materials. As the children are working, encourage them to share what they know about taking care of pets, such as feeding them, giving them water, talking to them, and petting them. Reinforce the concept of nonliving by asking the children if their "pets" need those things.

Caution: Be sure the rocks are large enough to prevent a choking hazard.

What are seeds?
What do seeds need to grow?

Caution: For activities on pages 19-20, use seeds and soil that have not been chemically treated. Closely supervise the children as they work with seeds to prevent a choking hazard.

Building Bridges: Seeds

Give each child a pumpkin seed. Encourage the children to describe what they see and guess what kind of seed it might be. Explain that inside every seed is a very tiny plant waiting to grow. There is enough food inside the seed to nourish the tiny plant until it begins to grow leaves.

I'm a Seed
(tune: "This Old Man")

I'm a seed. Watch me grow.
Which plant am I? I'd like to know.
Will I be a pumpkin or an apple tree?
Plant me and we'll wait and see.

Hey! You Forgot the Soil!

Most children assume that seeds need to be planted in soil to *germinate* (sprout). With the children's help, set up the following experiment:

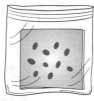

Materials:
- ☑ disposable cup
- ☑ zipper-top bag
- ☑ untreated potting soil
- ☑ bean or radish seeds
- ☑ water

Directions:
- ☼ Plant some seeds in a cup of untreated potting soil, about one inch down.
- ☼ Fold a few wet paper towels and lay them flat in a zipper-top bag. Place some seeds on the paper towels and seal the bag mostly closed.
- ☼ Place the cup and bag side by side on a windowsill and water them as needed.

Check the seeds every day for about two weeks. Both sets of seeds should begin to grow – proving that seeds do not need soil to germinate.

Note: Explore this concept further by showing the children pictures of *epiphytes* ("air plants") that grow in the rainforest.

What are seeds?
What do seeds need to grow?

Create Seed Mosaics

Show the children an example of a mosaic and point out how the pieces come together to form a picture. Set out construction paper, glue, and a variety of edible seeds. Invite the children to make their own mosaics by gluing the seeds onto paper.

Sort and Count Seeds

Preparation:

◊ Put three types of edible seeds into a small bag for each child. Choose seeds that are large enough for the children to sort and count (e.g., sunflower, pumpkin, bean).
◊ Give each child a bag and a sheet of paper divided into three columns.

Encourage the children to sort the seeds by type and place each in a separate column. Talk about the similarities and differences among the seeds. Count with the children to discover which column of seeds has the most and which has the least.

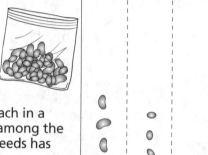

Experiment With Seeds

Have the children share their ideas about what seeds need to grow and record their thoughts on chart paper. With the children's help, set up the experiment described below. Encourage the children to predict which seeds will grow and write down their predictions. Check the seeds every day for about two weeks. Help the children compare their predictions with the results.

Materials:
- ☑ disposable cups labeled 1–5
- ☑ untreated potting soil
- ☑ bean or radish seeds
- ☑ water

Directions: Plant a few seeds in each cup of soil, about one inch down. Place the cups in the following locations and care for them as described:

- Refrigerator – Water as needed.
- Closed, dark box – Keep in a warm place, water as needed.
- Windowsill – Water as needed.
- Windowsill – Fill the cup with water.
- Windowsill – Do not water at all.

Variation: Do all seeds grow at the same rate? Conduct another experiment to find out. Plant more than one type of seed, each in its own cup. Label the cups, place them on the windowsill, and water as needed. Which seed sprouted first? Which took the longest to sprout?

What is the life cycle of a plant?

Building Bridges: Sequence the Life Cycle of a Plant

Preparation:

◊ Copy the "Life Cycle of a Plant" reproducible (p. 104).
◊ Cut apart the pictures and attach each one to a separate index card.
◊ Laminate the pictures or cover with contact paper.

Encourage the children to put the cards in order from the first step to the last. Once the cards are in order, help the children understand that a life cycle is like a circle. To demonstrate this concept, reorganize the cards so they flow in a circle.

Let's Pretend!

Describe the life cycle of a plant and invite the children to act it out. Have each child begin as a seed on the ground (squatting down and hugging knees), then turn off the lights (the sun).

○ It rains. A seed soaks up water and uses its stored food to grow. *(Teacher: Mist the "seeds" with water from a spray bottle.)*

○ First, the roots pop out. *Give a little hop while still hugging knees.*

○ Then the stem slowly curls up. *Slowly curl up into a standing position.*

○ Soon small leaves grow. *Put arms out to sides but keep elbows close to body.*

○ The leaves use sunlight to make food. *(Teacher: Turn on the lights.) Wiggle fingers.*

○ The leaves grow bigger. *Stretch arms out to sides.*

○ It rains. The roots soak up water. *(Teacher: Mist the "seeds" again.)*

○ Flower begins to grow. *Make circle above head with arms.*

○ The flowers spread their own seeds. *Pretend to be a seed and blow away in the wind.*

Little Seed, How Do You Grow?

(tune: "Twinkle, Twinkle Little Star")

Little seed, how do you grow?
I would really like to know.
    Water makes me swell and then,
    My roots pop out and I grow a stem.
    When my leaves stretch towards the sun,
    I make my food till the day is done.

Little plant, what happens next?
I would like to learn the rest.
    My flower blooms and then I will see,
    A butterfly or busy bee.
    Soon my seeds will blow away,
    And another plant will grow someday.

What do plants need to live and grow?

Building Bridges: Learn From an Expert

Invite a farmer (or avid gardener) to talk with your class about what farmers do to help their plants live and grow. Encourage the children to ask the "expert" questions that are important to them. After your guest leaves, have the children draw pictures about what they learned about growing plants.

Let's Pretend!

Include props in the Dramatic Play area to initiate role-play as farmers and gardeners (e.g., toy watering cans, hoes, shovels, wheelbarrows, gardening gloves). As the children explore, talk about what farmers and gardeners do to help their plants grow.

Experiment With Plants

Invite the children to share their ideas about what plants need to live, and record their thoughts on chart paper. With the children's help, set up the experiment described below. Encourage the children to predict which plant(s) will stay healthy and write down their predictions. Check the plants after about two weeks. Help the children compare their predictions with the results.

Materials:
- ☑ 5 identical green-leafed plants (same type and approximate size)
- ☑ water

Directions: Place the plants in the following locations and care for them as described:
- Dark closet or cabinet – Water as needed.
- Windowsill – Water as needed.
- Windowsill – Water too much.
- Windowsill – Do not water at all.
- Windowsill – "Water" as needed with soda.

Grow, Grow, Grow a Plant
(tune: "Row, Row, Row Your Boat")

Grow, grow, grow a plant
Show it that you care.
Give it water and some light
And share with it your air.

Did you know that plants provide us with the oxygen we need to breathe and remove excess carbon dioxide from our atmosphere?

Plants take in the carbon dioxide we breathe out, and we breathe in the oxygen that plants give off. Invite the children to "share their air" with a plant in your classroom.

What are the parts of a plant?

Building Bridges: Parts of a Plant

Draw a simple picture of a flowering plant including the flower, seeds, leaves, stem, and roots. Introduce the five main parts of a plant and briefly explain what each part does. Invite the children to stand and pretend they are plants as you sing the following song together:

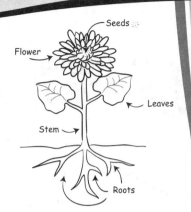

Parts of a Plant
(tune: "Head, Shoulders, Knees, and Toes")

As you sing, try adding the motions for each part of the plant!

Flower, seeds, leaves, stem, and roots,
Stem and roots.
Flower, seeds, leaves, stem, and roots,
Stem and roots.
Flower, seeds, leaves, stem, and roots.
Flower, seeds, leaves, stem, and roots,
Stem and roots.

Flower:	*Make a circle with arms above head.*
Seeds:	*Wiggle fingers in front of face.*
Leaves:	*Stretch arms out to the sides.*
Stem:	*Touch legs.*
Roots:	*Touch toes.*

Conduct an Experiment

Preparation:
◊ Gather three large plastic cups, food coloring, celery stalks with leaves, and white carnations.
◊ Prepare cups of red, blue, and green water. Add enough food coloring to make the color dark.
◊ Cut the bottoms of the celery and carnations on a slight angle.
◊ Put one stalk of celery and one carnation in each cup.

Encourage the children to predict what will happen to the celery and carnations, and record their ideas on chart paper. The next day, invite the children to examine the celery and carnations. The colored water should have traveled through the stem to the leaves/flowers. Cut open a stalk of celery and point out the tiny tubes inside. Explain that the tubes inside the stem carry the water to the rest of the plant.

Variation: Split the stem of one carnation in half lengthwise. Put half of the stem in one color and the other half in another color. Encourage the children to predict what will happen. (Both colors should travel through the stem to the flower.)

Are fruits and vegetables plants?

Building Bridges: Eat Plants

Many young children don't realize that when they eat fruits and vegetables, they are actually eating plants. Bring in a variety of fruits and vegetables for the children to explore with their senses. (You may want to prepare samples of each food ahead of time for the children to taste.)

Caution: Check with the children's families about potential food allergies.

Weigh Apples

Set out five or six apples. Hold up two of the apples. Have the children predict which of the two apples is heavier/lighter, then use a balance scale to test their predictions. Repeat this process several times, each time weighing a different pair of apples.

Play Hot Potato

Invite the children to sit in a circle. As you play recorded music, the children should gently but quickly pass a potato around the circle. (Tell the children to imagine that the potato is very hot!) When you stop the music, the child left holding the potato should stand up, move in a silly way, and sit back down. When you restart the music, the children should pass the potato again. Continue to play as long as the children show interest.

Toss and Catch Oranges

Divide the children into groups of three or four and have them stand in a circle. Provide each group with a plastic orange. Invite the children to gently toss the orange to each other.

Are trees and grass plants, too?

Caution: Before taking the children outside, explore the area yourself to see what is easily and safely accessible. Also, remember to check with families about potential outdoor allergies.

Building Bridges: Go on a Nature Walk

Take the children on a nature walk. Spend time observing the plant life and encourage the children to look for many different kinds of plants.

Choose a tree to explore. Talk about the parts of a tree: roots, trunk/stem, branches, leaves, flowers, and seeds. Collect leaves from a variety of trees. Encourage the children to examine the leaves and describe their similarities and differences.

Invite the children to sit in the grass. Show the children how to pick grass from the roots up. Point out the roots, stem (short thicker part near the root), and leaves (blades). Like grass, some plants do not grow flowers.

Go on a Scavenger Hunt

Create a checklist of plants and plant parts that can be found outside (e.g., leaves, grass, tree bark, acorns, flowers). Give each child a checklist and a small paper bag. Encourage the children to find the items on their lists and put them in their bags. Assist the children as needed. Invite the children to share and compare their treasures.

Note: As you create your checklist, use words and picture clues for each item the children are to find.

> **Variation:** Set out a large sheet of butcher paper. Invite the children to make a mural by gluing the items they found onto the paper. Title the mural "Our Plant Discoveries" and hang it at the children's eye level.

Paint With Plants

Invite the children to paint with leaves, twigs, and blades of grass. Encourage them to explore different movements and colors of paint as they work on their creations. Display the children's artwork after the paintings have dried.

Adopt a Tree

Choose a deciduous tree near your classroom to "adopt." (Deciduous trees drop their leaves as it gets colder.) Invite the children to make observations of "their tree" throughout the year. Encourage your young scientists to draw pictures of their tree in each season.

Many children have an affinity for animals. By beginning with pets, farm animals, and zoo animals, you can help the children connect their prior knowledge with new information about all sorts of creatures. As you are learning about each group of animals, display real-life pictures from books or the Internet whenever possible.

Caution: Before doing any of the outdoor activities in this section, check with the children's families about allergies to plants and animals that might be encountered outside.

Animals

How do you take care of a pet?

Building Bridges: Pets at Home

Each day, invite a few children to share how they take care of their pets at home. Encourage the children to bring in a drawing of their pet when it's their turn to share. For the children who do not have a pet at home, invite them to draw a picture of a pet they would like to have and share what they would do to take care of it. Display the children's artwork after each child has had an opportunity to share.

Graph Favorite Pets

Preparation:

◊ Draw four columns on chart paper to make a graph.
◊ Attach a picture of a pet at the bottom of each column.

Give each child a sticker. Invite the children to place the stickers above their favorite pets. Count with the children to discover which pet is liked the best and which is liked the least.

Do You Have a Pet?

(tune: "Do Your Ears Hang Low?")

Do you have a pet?
In your yard or in your house?
Do you have a cat, or a dog, or a mouse?
Do you feed it, give it water,
Do you love it through and through?
Like you need to do!

What animals live on a farm?
What animals live in a zoo?

Building Bridges: Farm and Zoo Animals

Preparation:

◊ Draw two columns on chart paper.
◊ Print "Farm Animals" on the top left and "Zoo Animals" on the top right.
◊ Draw or cut out pictures of farm and zoo animals.
◊ Attach each picture to a separate index card.

Encourage the children to name some farm animals and zoo animals. Display the picture cards and invite the children to decide if each animal would be found on a farm or in a zoo.

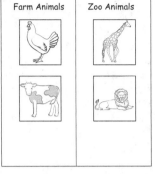

Variation: Set out several small plastic farm and zoo animals. Encourage the children to sort the animals in several different ways (e.g., farm/zoo, number of legs, type of animal).

Play Simon Says

Invite the children to play this variation of Simon Says. Begin all of your directions with, "Simon Says." Include both sounds and movements of farm and zoo animals. Challenge the children by including some incorrect directions. (They will enjoy hearing the teacher make such silly mistakes.) When the children hear an incorrect direction, they should "correct" the teacher. Use the examples below to help you get started.

Note: The request immediately following an incorrect direction should "fix" the problem that the children identified.

• Simon says ... moo like a cow	*Children start mooing.*
• Simon says ... gallop like a horse.	*Children stop mooing and start galloping.*
• Simon says ... fly like a giraffe.	*Children respond, "Hey! Giraffes don't fly!"*
• Simon says ... fly like a parrot.	*Children pretend to fly.*
• Simon says ... bark like a lion.	*Children respond, "Hey! Lions don't bark!"*
• Simon says ... roar like a lion.	*Children start roaring.*

Auntie's Farm and Uncle's Zoo

I like to visit my auntie's farm,
With the pig and the cow
And the big red barn.

I like to visit my uncle's zoo,
With the lion and the bear
And the kangaroo.

Old MacDonald
(traditional tune)

Old MacDonald had a farm.
E–I–E–I–O
And on his farm he had a pig.
E–I–E–I–O
With an oink, oink here.
And an oink, oink there.
Here an oink, there an oink,
Everywhere an oink, oink.
Old MacDonald had a farm.
E–I–E–I–O

And on his farm he had a cow…

And on his farm he had a horse…

And on his farm he had a sheep…

Make Paper Plate Pigs

Preparation:
◊ Cut circles and triangles out of pink construction paper.
◊ Set out the shapes, paper plates, glue, and other art materials.

Invite the children to decorate paper plates to look like pigs. The children may want to use a circle as the nose and triangles as the ears, or decorate their pigs in other ways.

> **Variation:** Share the traditional tale of *The Three Little Pigs*, then invite small groups of children to act out the story.

Play Cow, Cow, Horse

Ask the children to sit in a circle and choose one child to be It. It should walk around the circle and say "Cow" as he/she lightly taps each child on the shoulder. When It taps a child and says "Horse," the tapped child should gallop around the circle and try to tag It before It sits down in the empty spot. If It is tagged, he/she continues being It. If It sits before being tagged, the other child becomes It. Continue to play as long as the children show interest.

The Animals at the Zoo
(tune: "The Wheels on the Bus")

The monkeys at the zoo say ooo ooo ahh,
Ooo ooo ahh, ooo ooo ahh.
The monkeys at the zoo say ooo ooo ahh,
All day long!

The lions at the zoo say roar roar roar,
Roar roar roar, roar roar roar.
The lions at the zoo say roar roar roar,
All day long!

The bears at the zoo say grrr grrr grrr…

The snakes at the zoo say hiss hiss hiss…

The parrots at the zoo say squawk squawk squawk…

Play Musical Monkeys

Invite the children to stand in a circle and pretend that they are monkeys by making monkey movements and sounds. As you play recorded music, encourage the children to move around the circle like monkeys. When you stop the music, the children should quickly sit down in their spots. When you restart the music, the children should resume "monkeying" around the circle. Continue to play as long as the children show interest.

> **Variation:** Share the traditional fingerplay/story of *Five Little Monkeys Jumping on the Bed*.

Make Lion Puppets

Preparation:
◊ Cut yellow, orange, and brown yarn into 3–4 inch pieces.
◊ Set out the yarn, small paper bags, glue, and other art materials.

Invite the children to make lion puppets from paper bags. The children may want to create the lions' manes out of yarn or decorate their lions in other ways.

What is a habitat?

Building Bridges: Natural Habitats

A *habitat* is an animal's home, or where an animal lives. Explain to the children that some animals are kept and taken care of by people, such as pets, farm animals, and zoo animals, while others live in their natural habitats. Before exploring each of the following habitats, encourage the children to share what they already know about each one.

- "Backyard" (area around home/school)
- Wetlands (ponds/marshes)
- Forest
- Tropical rainforest
- Polar regions (Arctic and Antarctic)
- Ocean
- Savanna (tropical grasslands)
- Desert

A Habitat Is an Animal's Home
(tune: "The Ants Go Marching")

A habitat is an animal's home.
… A habitat!
A habitat is animal's home.
… A habitat!
A habitat is an animal's home –
Where they eat and sleep and play and roam.
There are many habitats!

Did You Ever See a Habitat?
(tune: "Did You Ever See a Lassie?")

Sing the verse(s) that you are learning about that day.

REFRAIN:
Did you ever see a habitat,
A habitat, a habitat?
Did you ever see a habitat
It's an animal's home!

REFRAIN
Did you ever see the wetlands,
The wetlands, the wetlands?
Did you ever see the wetlands
It's squishy and wet.

REFRAIN
Did you ever see a forest…
It's shady and green.

REFRAIN
Did you ever see a rainforest…
It's rainy and hot.

REFRAIN
Did you ever see the polar lands…
It's snowy and cold.

REFRAIN
Did you ever see an ocean…
It's salty and wet.

REFRAIN Did you ever see the savanna…
It's grassy and dry.

REFRAIN Did you ever see the desert…
It's sandy and hot.

What is a habitat?

Note: The activities on pages 33–35 are designed to help the children visualize various habitats. Using art to create "souvenirs" from each habitat, the children will construct their own experiences and images through which they can build upon prior knowledge about animals and their homes.

Draw What You See (Backyard)

Take the children outside to explore their "backyard" habitat. Set out plain white paper and encourage the children to draw pictures of the plants and animals they see. How do the animals use the plants in their habitat? What would happen to the animals if all the trees were cut down and all other plants removed? Explain that animals depend upon their habitat for shelter and food.

Note: The animals you find in your backyard habitat will vary depending upon where you live.

Paint With Watercolors (Wetlands)

Share a book about ponds and marshes and encourage the children to describe what they see. Invite the children to paint a pond scene with watercolor paints. As the children are working, talk about animals that live in the wetlands.

Pond Animals:

dragonfly	mallard duck	frog	beaver
trout	mosquito	painted turtle	muskrat

Make Leaf Rubbings (Forest)

Preparation:
◊ Have the children collect leaves in various shapes and sizes.
◊ Set out the leaves, paper, and unwrapped crayons.

Share a book about forests and encourage the children to describe what they see. Invite each child to choose a leaf and place it smooth side down under a sheet of paper. Show the children how to use the side of an unwrapped crayon to make a rubbing. As the children are working, talk about animals that live in the forest.

Forest Animals:

deer	bear	skunk	raccoon
owl	squirrel	rabbit	fox

What is a habitat?

Create Collages (Tropical Rainforest)

Share a book about tropical rainforests and encourage the children to describe what they see. Set out green tissue paper, brown and green chenille stems, and other art materials. Invite the children to create rainforest collages using the materials. The children may want to tear and crinkle the tissue paper to make the rainforest canopy or design their rainforests in other ways. As the children are working, play a rainforest recording in the background and talk about animals that live in the rainforest.

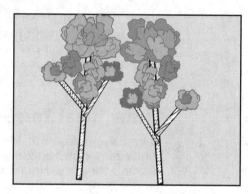

Rainforest Animals:

jaguar	spider monkey	boa constrictor	red-eyed tree frog
parrot	giant anteater	three-toed sloth	blue morpho butterfly

Design Icy Pictures (Polar Regions)

Preparation:

◊ Create a mixture of salt and sugar in a few bowls. (You could also add white or clear nonmetallic glitter to the mixture.)
◊ Set out the bowls, construction paper, and glue or glue sticks.

Share a book about the polar regions and encourage the children to describe what they see. As you are reading, point out the similarities and differences between the Arctic and Antarctic. Give each child an ice cube to explore. How does the ice cube feel? What do you think it would be like to live in the polar regions? Invite the children to design icy pictures by sprinkling the mixture over a light layer of glue on the paper. They may want to make pictures that look like snowdrifts and icebergs, or create other designs. As the children are working, talk about animals that live in the polar regions.

Polar Animals:

penguin	seal	polar bear	walrus
reindeer	Arctic fox	moose	beluga whale

What is a habitat?

Paint With Sponges (Ocean)

Share a book about oceans and encourage the children to describe what they see. Set out large sheets of white construction paper, blue paint, and sponges. Explain that there are animals called sponges that live in the ocean, which are similar to the sponges on the table. Invite the children to dip the sponges in paint and press them onto the paper. They may want to create an ocean scene or paint other designs. As the children are working, play a recording of ocean waves in the background and talk about other animals that live in the ocean.

Ocean Animals:

clam	puffer fish	sea star (starfish)	blue whale
lobster	seahorse	octopus	great white shark

Make Grassy Bracelets (Savanna)

Share a book about the savanna (tropical grasslands) and encourage the children to describe what they see. Help the children make masking tape bracelets. Loop the tape around each child's wrist with the sticky side of the tape away from the skin. Invite the children to cut pieces of raffia or tan yarn and stick it onto their bracelets. As the children are working, talk about animals that live in the tropical grasslands.

Savanna Animals:

lion	zebra	giraffe	rhinoceros
elephant	antelope	cheetah	hippopotamus

Design Sand Art (Desert)

Share a book about deserts and encourage the children to describe what they see. Give each child a small bowl of sand to explore. Invite the children to create designs with glue, then sprinkle sand on top. Have the children gently shake off the excess sand and set aside to dry. As the children are working, talk about animals that live in the desert.

Pond Animals:

coyote	camel	scorpion	desert tortoise
vulture	ostrich	rattlesnake	tarantula

Caution: Remind the children about safety when exploring sand (e.g., don't throw, don't rub eyes). Supervise closely as the children play.

What are mammals?

Building Bridges: Mammals

Show the children photographs of several different mammals. Encourage the children to describe what they see and share what they know about mammals. Use the following information to help facilitate the discussion:

- ☿ Some examples of mammals are: mouse, cat, monkey, deer, bat, elephant, and dolphin.
- ☿ Mammals have hair or fur.
- ☿ Most mammal babies are born alive.
  (Exceptions: The platypus and spiny anteater lay eggs.)
- ☿ Mammal babies drink milk from their mothers.
- ☿ Most mammals live on land.
  (See "The Biggest Animal of All!" on page 37 for exceptions.)

Explore Mammal Puzzles

Preparation:

- ◊ Draw or cut out pictures of several different mammals.
- ◊ Glue the pictures onto posterboard and set aside to dry.
- ◊ Laminate the pictures or cover with contact paper.
- ◊ Cut each picture into four pieces.

Give each child a puzzle piece. Invite the children to walk around and find the other three pieces to the puzzle. Once all the pieces have been found, the children should assemble the puzzle to reveal the mystery mammal.

Play Guess the Mammal

Display photographs of several different mammals around the classroom at the children's eye level (e.g., monkey, lion, rabbit, cow, mouse, elephant, whale). Encourage the children to walk around the classroom, closely observing the mammals' similarities and differences.

Have the children sit in a circle where they can still see the photographs. Tell the children that you are thinking of a mammal, and invite the children to guess what it is by asking "yes" or "no" questions. Since this type of questioning requires a great deal of practice, you may want to brainstorm some questions together before you begin. (See examples listed below.) Once a mammal is guessed or revealed, take down the photograph. Continue to play as long as the children show interest.

- ☿ Is the mammal big? Is it small?
- ☿ Does the mammal hop? Does it swim? Does it swing through the trees?
- ☿ Does the mammal live in the forest? Does it live in the ocean?
- ☿ Does the mammal roar? Does it moo? Does it squeak?
- ☿ Could I find the mammal on a farm? Could I find it in a zoo?

What are mammals?

The Biggest Animal of All!

Preparation:

◊ Measure and cut a 90-foot segment of yarn.
◊ Securely attach the yarn to the floor with clear tape.

The blue whale, measuring about 90 feet long, is the largest animal living today – and may be the largest animal to have ever lived! Many children think that whales are enormous fish, but they are actually mammals. Although most mammals live on land, some mammals, such as manatees and whales, live their entire lives in the water.

Invite the children to see just how big the biggest whale really is. Measure and cut yarn to the length of each child, and have the children compare their yarn segments to that of the blue whale. The children will surely have a "whale of a time" seeing how much larger blue whales are compared to them!

Note: A few mammals, such as seals, sea lions, walruses, and polar bears, spend their time both in the water and on land.

Variations: If you don't have enough inside space for a 90-foot long "blue whale," you could...
(1) Draw a 90-foot long line on the sidewalk with chalk.
(2) Cut a 30-foot long segment of yarn (or draw a 30-foot long chalk line) to represent an Orca whale instead.

Create Mammal Designs

Show the children photographs of mammals with distinct designs on their skin or fur (e.g., cheetah, tiger, zebra, giraffe, cow). Set out black, white, orange, tan, and brown construction paper. Invite the children to create mammal designs using the materials.

Make a Mammal Mural

Set out a large sheet of butcher paper, magazines, and a variety of art materials. Invite the children to draw or glue pictures of mammals onto the paper to make a mural. After the children finish, title it "Our Mammal Mural" and hang it at the children's eye level.

What are birds? Do all birds fly?

Building Bridges: Birds

Show the children photographs of several different birds. Encourage the children to describe what they see or share what they know about birds. Use the following information to help facilitate the discussion:

- Some examples of birds are: duck, eagle, cardinal, hummingbird, penguin, and ostrich.
- Birds have wings. (Exception: Bats also have wings, but bats are mammals.)
- Most birds fly. (Exceptions: The penguin, ostrich, and emu cannot fly.)
- A bird's skin is covered with feathers.
- Birds lay eggs.

Go Bird Watching

Spend some time outside bird watching. Listen to the different sounds that the birds make. Observe how they move. Do they all move in the same way? What colors are the birds? Encourage the children to make many observations of the birds in this "backyard" habitat, then set out plain paper and drawing materials. The children may choose to draw pictures of their observations.

Sort and Count Feathers

Preparation:

- Put three colors of craft feathers into a small zipper-top bag for each child.
- Give each child a bag and a sheet of paper divided into three columns.

Encourage the children to sort the feathers by color, placing each set of feathers in a separate column. Count with the children to discover which column of feathers has the most and which has the least.

 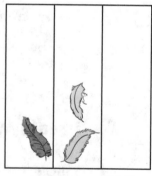

Paint With Feathers

Invite the children to paint with craft feathers. Encourage them to explore different movements and colors of paint as they work on their creations. Display each child's artwork after it has dried.

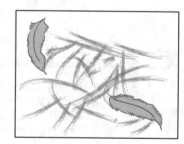

What are birds? Do all birds fly?

The Penguin Parade

Encourage the children to look closely at a photograph of a penguin and describe what they see. They may notice that the penguin's wings look like flippers. Some birds, like penguins, cannot fly. However, penguins use their wings to swim. While on land, penguins waddle or slide on the ice. Rockhopper penguins even bounce from ledge to ledge in their rocky habitat.

Invite the children to participate in a penguin parade. Line up the children one behind the other, and show them how to waddle like penguins: Keep your feet slightly apart and your legs straight. Keep your arms at your sides and flip your hands out. Now waddle from side to side like a penguin. Encourage the children to take turns being the leader in the penguin parade.

Count and Sing About Penguins

Preparation:
◊ Make ten copies of the "Penguin" reproducible (p. 107).
◊ Number the penguins from 1–10 and hang them at the children's eye level.

Help the children count the penguins as you point to each one. Count up from 1–10, then down from 10–1. Encourage the children to count along using their fingers as they sing the song below.

Ten Little Penguins
(tune: "Ten Little Indians")

1 little, 2 little, 3 little penguins,
4 little, 5 little, 6 little penguins,
7 little, 8 little, 9 little penguins,
10 penguins in a row!

10 little, 9 little, 8 little penguins,
7 little, 6 little, 5 little penguins,
4 little, 3 little, 2 little penguins,
1 penguin all alone!

Let's Pretend!

Encourage the children to describe how birds move, such as hopping, waddling, and flying. Invite the children to pretend to be birds. How many different kinds of birds can they pretend to be?

What are fish?

Building Bridges: Fish (Go Fishing)

Preparation:

◊ Cut fish shapes from posterboard.
◊ Print a fish fact on each cutout. (See examples below.)
◊ Securely tape a large paper clip to the mouth of each fish on the back.
◊ Make your own "fishing pole" by attaching a magnet on a string to the end of a ruler or wooden dowel.

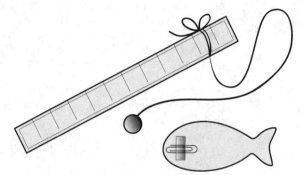

Invite the children to sit in a circle on the floor and imagine that they are going on a fishing trip. Encourage each child to "catch a fish" with the fishing pole. Read the fish fact to the children after each fish is caught. If you have more children than fish, throw them back into the pond after they are all caught. The second time a fish is caught, read the fact with a missing word or ask it in the form of a question. Encourage the children to fill in the blanks or answer the questions. Continue playing until all of the children have caught a fish. After the activity, show the children photographs of different kinds of fish (e.g., shark, swordfish, clownfish, puffer fish, goldfish).

Fish Facts:

🐠 Some fish live in freshwater while others live in <u>saltwater</u>.
🐠 You can find fish in <u>ponds, streams, rivers, lakes, and oceans</u>.
🐠 Fish use gills to breathe underwater. (What do fish use to breathe underwater?)
🐠 A fish's body is covered with <u>scales</u>.
🐠 A fish uses its fins and tail to help it swim. (What does a fish use to help it swim?)
🐠 Most fish lay <u>eggs</u>.
🐠 Many species of fish stay together in a group called a <u>school</u>.
🐠 A shark is a fish. (Is a shark a fish?)
🐠 A whale is not a fish. (Is a whale a fish?)

Create Tasty Fish Patterns

Give each child a small zipper-top bag of colored fish-shaped crackers. As the children watch, create a color pattern with the crackers. Invite the children to make their own color patterns and then eat them as a snack.

Note: Have the children wash their hands before doing this activity.

continued...

What are fish?

Let's Pretend!

Ask the children to show you how to make a fish face. Undoubtedly, many of the children will know how to make fish faces and will probably do so in unique ways. Enjoy this silly activity together by experimenting with the fish faces that the children share. Pretend you are a school of fish swimming around in the ocean.

Decorate Fish

Set out paper plates, wiggly eyes, and other art materials. Invite the children to create and design fish. Have each child cut a triangular section from a paper plate to make a mouth, and glue or tape the section across from where it was cut to make a tail. Encourage the children to decorate their fish as desired.

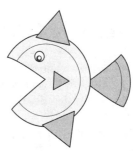

Measure With Fish

Have each child trace one hand on a sheet of paper with his/her fingers widely spread. Give each child a small bowl of fish-shaped crackers. Encourage the children to estimate how many fish wide their hands are (from pinky to thumb). Have the children measure with the fish-shaped crackers to see if their estimations were correct. Once they are done measuring, invite the children to enjoy a fishy snack.

Explore Lacing Cards

Preparation:
◊ Cut fish shapes out of heavy posterboard.
◊ Use a hole punch to make a series of holes around each fish.
◊ For each lacing card, tie a string through one hole to anchor it. (Be sure the string is long enough to reach around the fish twice.)

Invite the children to practice lacing the string in and out of the holes. This skill requires some practice, so assist the children as needed.

What are reptiles?

Building Bridges: Reptiles

Show the children photographs of some reptiles. Encourage the children to describe what they see or share what they know about reptiles. Use the following information to help facilitate the discussion:

- Some examples of reptiles are: crocodile, alligator, turtle, tortoise, snake, and lizard.
- Reptiles have tough, dry skin or scales.
- Most reptiles lay eggs. (Exception: Some snakes are born alive.)
- Reptiles can live in the water or on land, but still breathe air with their lungs.

Compare Crocodiles and Alligators

Preparation:
◊ Draw a Venn diagram (two overlapping circles) on a large sheet of butcher paper.
◊ Print "Crocodile" above the left circle and "Alligator" above the right circle.

Show the children photographs of crocodiles and alligators. Encourage the children to describe what they see or share what they know about each animal. How are they the same? How are they different? Write the similarities in the overlapping area between the two circles and the differences across from each other in the outer parts of the circles. Provide additional information as needed. An example of a Venn diagram is shown below to help you get started.

Crocodile   **Alligator**

Crocodile	(shared)	Alligator
narrow, pointed snout	reptiles	broad, rounded snout
olive-brown color	lay eggs	blackish color
teeth of both jaws are visible when mouth is closed	tough scales	only teeth of upper jaw are visible when mouth is closed
usually found in saltwater	dangerous	usually found in freshwater

What are reptiles?

Slow and Steady Wins the Race

Tortoises are very slow animals, yet one tortoise still found a way to win a race! Share this fable with the children, and then talk about the moral of the story. Its origins are credited to the Greek storyteller, Aesop. Use your favorite version or the one below.

The Tortoise and the Hare

One day, a young and energetic hare was bragging to the other animals. "I am surely faster than any of you!" he boasted. And, as usual, the hare challenged the other animals to a race. The old tortoise was getting tired of hearing the boastings and braggings of the hare, and accepted the challenge. The hare couldn't believe his ears! The tortoise and the hare in a race? Even the other animals thought it was a silly idea; but they, too, were sick of listening to the hare.

The tortoise and the hare stood at the starting line and the race began. The hare scampered off as fast as he could go. There was no way he was going to let the tortoise beat him in a race! The tortoise, on the other hand, slowly plodded along as the other animals cheered.

Not long after the race began, the hare found himself very close to the finish line. The hare looked back and saw that the tortoise was still very far away. "I am so much faster than he is," he thought, "I should just lie down here and take a nap. The tortoise will never catch up to me." And he did. While the hare was sleeping, the tortoise continued to mosey his way toward the finish line.

Quite some time later, the hare woke up from his long, restful nap. And what do you think he saw? The tortoise won the race! The hare could hardly believe it. "How could this happen?" the hare wondered. "Slow and steady wins the race," lectured the tortoise. "Slow and steady wins the race."

Let's Pretend!

Reinforce sequencing skills by reviewing the fable of "The Tortoise and the Hare," then invite the children to act out the story. All the children can be animals, so every child can have a role to play!

Slow and Steady

(tune: "Yankee Doodle")

"Slow and steady wins the race,"
The tortoise told the hare.
"You stay on track and keep your pace
And that will get you there."

"Keep on keeping on, you see –
That's the way to do it.
Learn a lesson now from me –
Don't rush, don't stop, and don't quit!"

Have you ever wondered what the difference is between turtles and tortoises? Scientifically, they are a part of the same family, but they are commonly distinguished from each other in the following way: Turtles spend much of their time in the water, while tortoises spend all of their time on land.

What are reptiles?

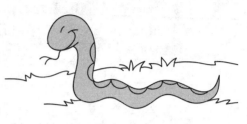

Building Bridges: Snakes

Show the children photographs of snakes in various colors and sizes. Encourage the children to describe what they see or share what they know about snakes. Use the following information to help facilitate the discussion:

- A snake's skin is covered with scales. Although they look slimy, their scales are actually very dry.
- Snakes are carnivores. They eat other animals, such as small mammals, eggs, and even other snakes.
- A snake must shed its skin as it grows.
- Snakes "smell" with their forked tongues.

Make Paper Plate Snakes

Preparation:

- Draw a spiral on a paper plate beginning on the outside and ending on the inside of the plate.
- Set out the paper plates, washable-ink pads, wiggly eyes, and other art materials.

Invite the children to design snakes using the materials. After the children cut along the spiral on the paper plate, they may choose to make fingerprint "scales" or decorate their snakes in other ways. Assist the children as needed.

Toss Beanbags

Preparation:

- Draw a large, wiggly snake with stripes on butcher paper.
- Color each section of the snake a different color.
- Securely tape the snake to the floor with clear tape.

Invite the children to stand in a circle around the snake. Give one child a beanbag to toss onto the snake. The child who tossed the beanbag should name the color on which the beanbag landed, then move in a silly way. All children wearing the color that was named should move in the same way as the first child. Continue to play until all the children have had an opportunity to toss the beanbag.

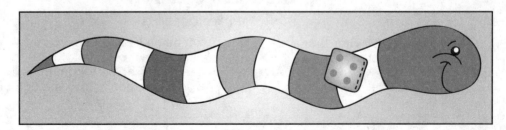

What are amphibians?

Building Bridges: Amphibians

Show the children photographs of several species of frogs, toads, and salamanders. Encourage the children to describe what they see or share what they know about amphibians. Use the following information to help facilitate the discussion:

- All amphibians begin their lives in the water and breathe underwater with their gills.
- As amphibians become adults, they develop lungs and breathe air.
- Amphibians lay eggs.
- Some amphibians live on land, but must return to the water to lay their eggs. Other amphibians spend most of their time in the water, but they still breathe air with their lungs.

The Small Frog

(rhythm: "Little Miss Muffet")

Near the wet, swampy bog
There sat a small frog
Waiting for a meal to eat.
Soon he did spy
A tasty, old fly…
Oh! What a nice little treat!

Play Red Light, Green Light

Show the children how to jump like frogs. Spread your feet apart and squat low to the ground. Place your hands on the ground in front of you. Use your legs to spring up and forward, and then come back down into a squat. Allow time for the children to practice jumping like frogs.

Invite your little "froggies" to play Red Light, Green Light. The children should form a line shoulder to shoulder with some space between them. Stand about 30 feet away on a line parallel with the children. When you say, "Green light!" the children should shout "Go!" and jump toward you like frogs. When you say, "Red light!" they should shout "Stop!" and then freeze. Alternate directions until all of the children have jumped to the line on which you are standing.

What are amphibians?

Sequence the Life Cycle of a Frog

Preparation:
◊ Copy the "Life Cycle of a Frog" reproducible (p. 105).
◊ Cut apart the pictures and attach each one to a separate index card.
◊ Laminate the pictures or cover with contact paper.

Encourage the children to put the cards in order from the first step to the last. Once the cards are in order, help the children understand that a life cycle is like a circle. To demonstrate this concept, reorganize the cards so they flow in a circle.

Make Frog Faces From Circles

Set out green and white construction paper, glue or tape, and black markers. Have the children cut out one large green circle (head), two small white circles (outer part of eyes), and two even smaller green circles (inner part of eyes). Invite the children to use these shapes to make frog faces.

Note: You may want to give the children circles cut from posterboard to trace.

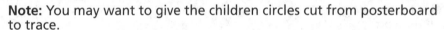

The Frogs Near the Pond
(tune: "The Wheels on the Bus")

The mother frog lays many eggs,
Many eggs, many eggs.
The mother frog lays many eggs,
In the pond.

The tadpoles hatch and stick to plants,
Stick to plants, stick to plants.
The tadpoles hatch and stick to plants,
In the pond.

Tiny tadpoles breathe through gills,
Breathe through gills, breathe through gills.
Tiny tadpoles breathe through gills,
In the pond.

Hind legs grow and then the front,
Then the front, then the front.
Hind legs grow and then the front,
In the pond.

Now the young frogs breathe with lungs,
Breathe with lungs, breathe with lungs.
Now the young frogs breathe with lungs,
In the pond.

Once the frogs' tails disappear,
Disappear, disappear,
Once the frogs' tails disappear,
They hop out!

The frogs near the pond go hop hop hop,
Hop hop hop, hop hop hop.
The frogs near the pond go hop hop hop,
All day long!

What are animal babies called?

Building Bridges: Match Animal Parents and Babies

Preparation:
- ◊ Copy the "Animal Babies" reproducible (p. 108) and mount on posterboard.
- ◊ You may want to color the animals, as well.
- ◊ Laminate the pictures or cover with contact paper.
- ◊ Cut apart the pictures.

Lay the cards faceup on a table or the floor. Invite the children to match the parents with their babies by looking at the pictures. Introduce the names of the babies after each match is made.

> **Variation:** Use the animal cards to play a matching game. Place the cards facedown. Each player flips over two cards on his/her turn. A match is made when a parent and its baby are revealed. If a match is not made, the cards are flipped back over and it is the next player's turn. Players continue to take turns until all the matches have been made.

Animal Babies

As you share this rhyme, encourage the children to listen for the animal babies.

Bears and lions and cheetahs, too,
Should teach their <u>cubs</u> just what to do.
Of course, the whale in the deep blue sea,
Should teach its <u>calf</u> just how to be.

A dog should surely teach its <u>pup</u>
What to do when it grows up.
A goose should teach its little one
What <u>goslings</u> do to have some fun.

<u>Kids</u> and <u>kittens</u>, and <u>fawns</u> and <u>foals</u>,
And <u>chicks</u> and <u>joeys</u> and tiny <u>tadpoles</u>,
All need their parents to help them grow,
And show them what they need to know.

What are some animals that live in the ocean?

Building Bridges: Ocean Animals

Children learn quickly that there are fish in the ocean, but what about the other unique creatures in the sea? Animals such as clams, oysters, crabs, lobsters, octopuses (also called octopi), jellyfish, sea stars (starfish), sponges, and sea anemones all live in the ocean. Show the children photographs of some ocean animals. Encourage the children to describe what they see or share what they know about each one.

Trace and Cut Sea Stars

Cut star patterns in several sizes out of cardstock. Invite the children to trace the patterns on the back side of sandpaper and cut them out. Assist the children as needed.

Note: Although most people call these animals starfish, scientists prefer to call them sea stars because they are not actually fish.

Dance Like an Octopus

Preparation:

◊ Cut streamers into 1-foot sections. (You will need eight streamers for each child.)
◊ Set out paper plates, tape or glue, and the streamers.

Invite each child to make an octopus by attaching eight streamers (tentacles) to a paper plate. After all the children have made their octopuses, play a recording of ocean sounds as the children do an octopus dance.

Sea Creatures

I want to take a trip
To the bottom of the sea,
And explore all the animals there.

Like lobsters, and clams,
And jellyfish there'll be –
No other creatures compare!

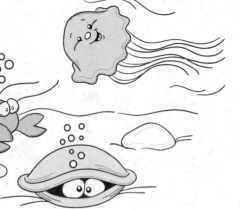

What are insects?

Inspect Insects

Take the children outside to find some friendly (harmless) insects, such as ladybugs, crickets, grasshoppers, and black ants. Invite the children to examine the insects they find with magnifying glasses and/or draw pictures to record their observations.

Note: Some children are uncomfortable around insects, so consider offering an alternative to this activity, such as creating insects out of clay.

Caution: Check with the children's families about potential allergies. Also, discuss safety issues with the children (e.g., staying away from insects that sting).

Building Bridges: Insects

Show the children photographs of insects with which they are familiar (e.g., ladybug, firefly, mosquito, butterfly, bee, ant, dragonfly). Encourage the children to describe what they see or share what they know about insects. Use the following information to help facilitate the discussion:

- Insects are everywhere – from the coldest polar regions to the hottest tropical rainforests!
- There are more species of insects than all the other animals in the world combined!
- Insects hatch from tiny eggs. Some insects look like miniature adults when they hatch, while others change completely (metamorphosis).
- All insects have a body divided into three main parts, six legs, and a hard outer covering (exoskeleton). Most insects have wings (one or two pair) and two *antennae* (an-TEN-ay).
- Although many people call insects "bugs," true bugs are a type of insect. That means that all bugs are insects, but not all insects are bugs.

Ladybug

Ladybug, ladybug
Red and black
Where are you going?
When will you come back?

Firefly

Firefly, firefly
Quick and bright
Where are you going on
This lovely summer night?

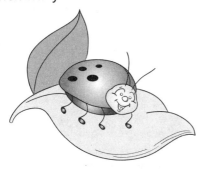

What are insects?

Ants at a Picnic

What do you picture when you think of ants at a picnic? Most people probably imagine ants getting into their food. In this activity, the children will "invite" the ants to their own little picnic!

- Encourage the children to predict what ants like to eat and don't like to eat, and record their thoughts on chart paper.
- Choose three or four foods from their list to set out for the ants' picnic, intentionally selecting at least one food ants will like (e.g., apple) and one they probably won't (e.g., pickle).
- Have the children help break the foods into tiny pieces and place each food on its own paper plate.
- Set the paper plates outside away from the building. About an hour or so later, take the children outside to see which food(s) the ants really liked best!
- Help the children compare their predictions to the results.

Caution: Have the children observe the ants from a distance to prevent bites.

The Insect Song

(tune: "She'll Be Coming Round the Mountain")

You can find some insects anywhere you look.
You can find some insects anywhere you look.
Under rocks and in the air,
Over here and over there.
You can find some insects anywhere you look.

Did you know they have six legs and most have wings?
Did you know they have six legs and most have wings?
They can crawl or they can fly,
They can climb up really high.
Did you know they have six legs and most have wings?

Oh their bodies are divided in three parts.
Oh their bodies are divided in three parts.
That's how you can start to tell
If they're insects, really well.
Oh their bodies are divided in three parts.

How does a caterpillar become a butterfly?

Building Bridges:
Sequence the Life Cycle of a Butterfly

Preparation:
◊ Copy the "Life Cycle of a Butterfly" reproducible (p. 106).
◊ Cut apart the pictures and attach each one to a separate index card.
◊ Laminate the pictures or cover with contact paper.

Encourage the children to put the cards in order from the first step to the last. Once the cards are in order, help the children understand that a life cycle is like a circle. To demonstrate this concept, reorganize the cards so they flow in a circle.

Let's Pretend!

Describe the life cycle of a butterfly and invite the children to act it out. Have each child begin as an egg on a leaf.

An egg is laid on a leaf.	*Squat down and hug knees.*
A tiny caterpillar hatches from the egg.	*Pretend to break through the egg.*
The caterpillar eats MANY leaves and begins to grow.	*Pretend to eat.*
The caterpillar hangs from a twig and forms a hard outer shell around itself called a chrysalis.	*Stand up and give yourself a hug.*
About two weeks later… A beautiful butterfly wiggles out of its chrysalis...	*Say or sing the days of the week twice. Wiggle a bit and spread out wings.*
Flutters from flower to flower…	*Flutter around the room.*
And drinks nectar with its long tongue.	*Pretend to land on a flower and "drink" with tongue.*

Create Caterpillars

Set out pom-poms, glue, wiggly eyes, and other art materials. Invite the children to create caterpillars by gluing the pom-poms together in a chain. They may want to cut leaves out of construction paper for the caterpillars "to eat," as well.

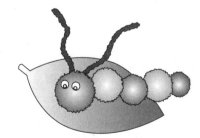

How does a caterpillar become a butterfly?

Order Butterflies

Cut five or six butterfly shapes from posterboard in various colors and sizes. Scatter the butterflies on a table or the floor. Encourage the children to order the butterflies from smallest to biggest. Scatter the butterflies again, this time asking the children to order the butterflies from biggest to smallest.

Design Butterflies

Preparation:

◊ Gather a few spray bottles and fill them with water.
◊ Cut chenille stems into 6-inch segments.
◊ Set out coffee filters, washable markers, chenille stem segments, and other art materials.

Invite the children to design butterflies by coloring the coffee filters with markers.

☼ Once they are finished coloring, the children may choose to lightly mist their filters with a spray bottle to allow the colors to spread and blend together.
☼ After the filters dry, help each child pinch the filter in the middle and wrap it with a chenille stem. The ends of the chenille stem can then be curled to create antennae.
☼ Hang the children's butterflies around the room to display their artwork.

Flitter, Flutter

Flitter, flutter...
The butterfly flies from flower to flower.

Flitter, flutter...
The butterfly hides from a light rain shower.

Flitter, flutter...
The butterfly spreads her beautiful wings.

Flitter, flutter...
The butterfly dances, the butterfly sings.

What are some differences between a butterfly and a moth?

Butterflies fly mostly during the day, have thin bodies and antennae with knobs at the ends, and form a chrysalis as they change from a caterpillar to a butterfly.

Moths fly mostly at night, have thicker bodies and antennae without knobs, and form a cocoon as they change from a caterpillar to a moth.

What are spiders?
Are spiders insects?

Building Bridges: Spiders

Show the children photographs of spiders. Encourage the children to describe what they see or share what they know about spiders. Use the following information to help facilitate the discussion:

- Spiders are not insects.
- Spiders' bodies are divided into two parts. (Insects have three.)
- Spiders have eight legs. (Insects have six.)
- Spiders do not have wings or antennae. (Most insects do have wings and antennae.)
- Daddy longlegs are not spiders. (However, daddy longlegs and spiders are both arachnids.)

Spider Snacks

Give each child one small rice cake, one large rice cake, a spoonful of low-fat cream cheese, eight thin pretzel sticks, and a paper plate. Invite the children to create their own healthy spider snacks by following the steps listed below. As the children are working, remind them that spiders are NOT insects. The easiest way to tell is to count their legs – insects have six and spiders have eight. Encourage the children to count the legs on their spiders before they eat them.

- Lay the rice cakes side by side on a plate.
- Use a small amount of cream cheese to stick the rice cakes together.
- Attach the pretzel sticks to the large rice cake with cream cheese to make legs (four on each side).

The Itsy, Bitsy Spider
(traditional tune)

The itsy, bitsy spider
Went up the waterspout.
Down came the rain
And washed the spider out.
Out came the sun
And dried up all the rain.
Then the itsy, bitsy spider
Went up the spout again.

Wiggle fingers up.

Wiggle fingers down.
Cross arms with palms down. ("Safe!" sign)
Circle arms above head.

Wiggle fingers up.

Variation: Invite the children to illustrate new adventures with the itsy, bitsy spider on plain white paper. Cover the pages with construction paper and staple along the edge to make a class book.

What are earthworms?

Search for Earthworms

Preparation:

◊ Gather disposable cups, digging tools (e.g., spoons and toy shovels), magnifying glasses, and drawing materials.

◊ Locate an area outside with many earthworms, or "plant" some in the soil if necessary.

Take the children outside to search for earthworms. Invite the children to examine the worms they find with magnifying glasses and/or draw pictures to record their observations.

Note: Some children are uncomfortable touching worms or digging in dirt. You may want to offer an alternative to this activity, such as exploring books about earthworms.

Building Bridges: Earthworms

Invite the children to sit in a circle and bring along their earthworms. Encourage the children to share their earthworm discoveries and compare their worms side by side. Which worm is the longest? Which is the shortest? Which is the fattest? Which is the skinniest? How do worms move? Do you think a worm can see and hear? Why or why not? Use the following information to help facilitate the discussion:

- Earthworms "hatch" from an *egg cocoon* (also called an egg case).
- An earthworm's body is divided into parts called segments.
- Earthworms have a "head" end (pointy end where the mouth is located) and a "tail" end (but no tail).
- An earthworm moves by wiggling its body in waves from the head end to the tail end. Its segments expand and contract as it moves.
- Earthworms eat soil, leaves, and other decaying plant matter. As they eat, earthworms make tunnels through the dirt.
- Earthworms breathe through their skin.
- Earthworms do not have eyes but can sense light, and do not have ears but can sense vibrations. They use these senses to help keep them away from danger (e.g., drying out in the sun or being eaten by a bird).

Note: After they share their earthworm discoveries, have the children wash their hands.

Earthworm, Earthworm

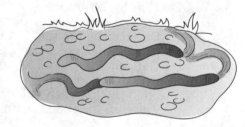

Earthworm, earthworm on the ground,
Tunnel through the dirt so you can't be found.
Here comes a robin singing her song,
She's looking for a bite to eat and hopping right along.
Earthworm, earthworm on the ground,
Tunnel through the dirt so you can't be found.

What are earthworms?

Explore Playdough

Invite the children to make worms by rolling playdough between their hands or on a table. Challenge them to make skinny worms and fat worms, short worms and long worms. Encourage the children to talk about and compare their worms as they explore the playdough.

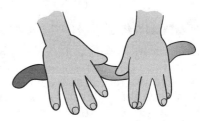

Wiggle Like Worms

Invite the children to wiggle like earthworms on the floor by keeping their arms at their sides and their legs together. Challenge the children to move toward a specific destination by wiggling their bodies from head to toe.

Wiggle Worm

(tune: "Mary Had a Little Lamb")

**Each time you sing the song,
fill in a different child's name.**

_____ is a wiggle worm,
Wiggle worm, wiggle worm!
_____ is a wiggle worm,
Watch him/her wiggle now!   *Child wiggles.*

Paint With "Worms"

Set out construction paper, dishes of paint, and "worms" (e.g., plastic fishing lures, pieces of yarn). Invite the children to paint by moving their worms over the paper, exploring different movements and colors of paint. Display the children's artwork after the paintings have dried.

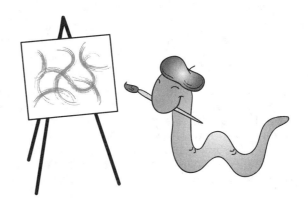

How do animals protect themselves?

Building Bridges: Animal Defenses

Animals must find ways to protect themselves from their enemies. An animal might move quickly to get away, use camouflage to hide, stay with a group for protection, or use its body parts to warn or hurt its enemy. Display several photographs of animals (see examples below) and have the children explain how each animal protects itself. Use the following information to help facilitate the discussion:

- Elephants – stay together in a group (herd)
- Snakes – some are poisonous, rattlesnakes use noise to scare away enemies (shake tail)
- Skunks – give off a terrible odor
- Monkeys – swing from branch to branch, use camouflage to blend in with surroundings
- Poison dart frogs – warn predators with bright colors, excrete poison
- Turtles – hide in their shells
- Porcupines – curl up into a ball and stick spines out
- Crocodiles – swat with tail, have very sharp teeth
- Lizards – run away quickly, some can lose their tail (and still live)
- Eagles – use sharp beak and talons, fly away

Move Like Animals

One way animals protect themselves is to get away from their enemies (predators). Brainstorm ways that animals move and make a list on chart paper. After each word is shared, invite the children to move in that way. For example, if someone says "swim," have the children pretend to swim. The following are some moving words to help you get started:

climb	hop	scamper	stomp	crawl
jump	slither	swim	creep	leap
sneak	swing	fly	paddle	soar
waddle	gallop	prance	sprint	wiggle

Play Animal Charades

Preparation:

- ◊ Draw or cut out pictures of animals that move in different ways.
- ◊ Attach each picture to a separate index card.
- ◊ Place the cards in an opaque container so the children cannot see the cards inside.

Explain to the children that while playing charades you cannot make any sounds. Invite the children, one at a time, to pick a card from the container and move like the animal on the card without making a sound. The other children should try to guess the animal. If you have more children than cards, put the cards back into the container once all of them have been drawn. Continue until everyone has had a chance to play.

How do animals protect themselves?

Explore Camouflage

Preparation:

◊ Cut a few 2-inch squares from red felt.
◊ Cut several 2-inch squares from green and brown felt.
◊ Lay the felt pieces in the grass, spacing them at least a few feet apart.

Camouflage allows an animal to blend into its surroundings. Use the following hands-on activity to explore camouflage. Have the children stand along the perimeter of the area you prepared. Without moving, encourage the children to glance quickly around the area and count the pieces of felt that they can see. Which color was the easiest to find? Why were the brown and green pieces harder to find? Next, have the children walk around to find all the felt pieces. They may be surprised to find that there were more green and brown pieces, even though they were harder to see.

Hey There, Animal...

(tune: "Baa, Baa, Black Sheep")

**For each verse, fill in the appropriate animal.
Try adding motions as you sing!**

Hey there, <u>monkey</u>
What is it you do
To keep yourself safe
So no one eats you?
   <u>I swing through the branches from tree to tree</u>,
   <u>Very few animals can ever catch me</u>.
Thank you, <u>monkey</u>
For telling what you do
To keep yourself safe
So no one eats you.

Hey there, tortoise...
   I pull my head and legs inside,
   In my shell, is where I hide.

Hey there, skunk...
   I raise my tale up to the sky,
   Then my stink will make you cry.

Hey there, rabbit...
   Camouflage makes me hard to see,
   But if I'm found I'll hop and flee.

What does extinct mean?
What does endangered mean?

Building Bridges: Extinct and Endangered Animals

Introduce the words *extinct* and *endangered* to the children. If an animal is extinct, it means that there are no more animals of its kind living today. If an animal is endangered, it means that the number of animals is decreasing and they are in danger of becoming extinct.

Most young children are familiar with dinosaurs, which became extinct millions of years ago. However, many less-familiar animals, such as the Dodo (a type of bird), Quagga (related to the zebra and horse), and Caspian tiger, have just become extinct within the past few hundred years. Below is a list of extinct and endangered animals that might interest the children. Explore the Internet and other resources for more information.

Extinct:
- Dodo
- Quagga
- Caspian tiger
- Saber-toothed tiger
- American mastodon
- Woolly mammoth
- Giant ground sloth
- Dinosaurs (see pp. 60–63 for dinosaur activities)
- Plesiosaurus (marine reptile, not a dinosaur)
- Pterodactyl (flying reptile, not a dinosaur)

Endangered:
- Bald eagle
- American alligator
- Gray wolf
- Green sea turtle
- Sea otter
- Chimpanzee
- Lemur
- Three-toed sloth
- Jaguar
- African elephant

Create With Clay

Invite the children to make models of their favorite endangered animals out of air-drying clay. Encourage the children to share their creations with the class and talk about the animals they created.

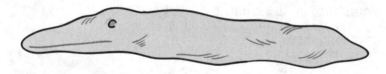

Where, Oh, Where Did the Dodo Go?

(tune: "Where, Oh, Where Has My Little Dog Gone?")

Where, oh, where did the dodo go?
Oh where, oh where could it be?
The dodo bird is now extinct –
There are no more to see.

Where, oh, where did the mammoth go?
Oh where, oh where could it be?
The woolly mammoth is now extinct –
There are no more to see.

What are fossils?

Building Bridges: Fossils

If possible, bring in a real fossil for the children to examine. Explain that a fossil can be a plant or animal or an imprint of a plant or animal that turned into rock over millions of years. People who search for and study fossils are called *paleontologists* (PAY-lee-on-**TAHL**-uh-jists). Paleontologists use special tools to help them find fossils. They must also work carefully and patiently so they do not break the fossils as they are searching for them. Share a book with the children about fossils.

Find Fossils

Preparation:
◊ Hide medium-sized rocks in a sandbox or sand table.
◊ Set out dry paintbrushes and craft sticks for the children to use as tools.

Invite small groups of children to find "fossils" in the sand. Encourage the children to carefully move the sand using the tools to reveal the hidden fossils. Ask the children to find one "fossil" then allow another child to have a turn.

Make Fossil Imprints

Remind the children that a fossil can be an imprint of a plant or an animal from a long time ago. Set out air-drying clay and a variety of plant parts (e.g., leaves, twigs, bark, pinecones). Invite the children to make their own fossil imprints by firmly pressing items into the clay. Remove the items and allow the "fossils" to dry overnight.

Variation: Create imprints of a variety of items in clay or playdough, such as a coin, key, pencil, fork, and paper clip. Place the imprints and the items on a table or tray, and invite the children to match each item to its "fossil."

I Want to Find a Fossil

I want to find a fossil
In my very own backyard.
I dig and dig for fossils,
But finding them is hard.
I'd like to find a fossil
Of a great big dinosaur…
Or even just a tiny plant
That no one's found before.

What were dinosaurs?

Building Bridges: Animal Defenses

Show the children several pictures of dinosaurs. Explain that dinosaurs were reptiles that lived millions of years ago. Encourage the children to describe what they see or share what they already know about dinosaurs. Use the following information to help facilitate the discussion:

- Dinosaurs were reptiles. Like most reptiles, dinosaur babies hatched from eggs.
- Some dinosaurs were as small as chickens (e.g., Compsognathus) and some were as big as buildings (e.g., Brachiosaurus)!
- Some dinosaurs, such as the Apatosaurus, were herbivores (they only ate plants).
- Most of these dinosaurs walked slowly on four legs.
- Some dinosaurs, such as the Tyrannosaurus rex, were carnivores (they only ate meat).
- Most of these dinosaurs moved quickly on two legs.
- Scientists learned about the body structure of many dinosaurs by rebuilding their skeletons from fossilized bones. However, dinosaurs' skin textures and colors are still left open to the imagination.
- Dinosaurs are extinct. There are no more dinosaurs alive today.

Note: There are four common misconceptions you may need to correct:
(1) Not all dinosaurs were big.
(2) Not all dinosaurs were "mean" and dangerous.
(3) Pterodactyls and plesiosaurs were not dinosaurs, but they did live during the same time period.
(4) The true name of the "brontosaurus" is Apatosaurus.

Pronunciation Key:		
	Apatosaurus	(uh-PAT-uh-**SORE**-uhs)
	Brachiosaurus	(BRAK-ee-uh-**SORE**-uhs)
	Compsognathus	(komp-**SAHG**-nuh-thus)
	Spinosaurus	(SPINE-uh-**SORE**-uhs)
	Stegosaurus	(STEG-uh-**SORE**-uhs)
	Triceratops	(try-**SEHR**-uh-tops)
	Tyrannosaurus rex	(tie-RAN-uh-**SORE**-uhs reks)
	Pterodactyl	(tare-uh-**DAK**-tuhl)
	Plesiosaur	(**PLEE**-zee-uh-SORE)

Design Dinosaurs

Set out different colors of clay or playdough and invite the children to create their own unique dinosaurs. They can be models of dinosaurs that really existed or created from their own imaginations. Invite the children to talk about their dinosaurs when they are finished.

What were dinosaurs?

Play Dino Bingo

Preparation:

◊ Make copies of the "Dino Bingo" reproducible (p. 109).
◊ Display pictures of the following dinosaurs: Apatosaurus, Brachiosaurus, Spinosaurus, Stegosaurus, Triceratops, and Tyrannosaurus rex.

Encourage the children to look closely at the dinosaur pictures.

- Talk about some distinct features of these dinosaurs (e.g., Tyrannosaurus rex had very sharp teeth, Triceratops had three big horns).
- Give each child a bingo sheet, scissors, and glue. Invite the children to cut out nine dinosaurs and glue one in each box on the bingo sheet.
- As the children play, remind them to only cover one dinosaur each time.
- Continue to play until all of the children get Bingo (three in a row in any direction).

Graph Favorite Dinosaurs

Preparation:

◊ Draw four columns on chart paper to make a graph.
◊ Attach a picture of a dinosaur at the bottom of each column.

Give each child a sticker. Invite the children to place the stickers above their favorite dinosaurs. Count with the children to discover which dinosaur is liked best and which is liked the least.

Make Dinosaur Counting Books

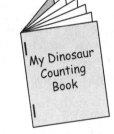

Preparation:

◊ Cut several sheets of 8½" x 11" paper to make pieces that are 8½" x 5½".
◊ For each child, fold three of the pieces of paper in half and staple along the edge to make a book.
◊ Print "My Dinosaur Counting Book" on the front of each book.

Beginning on the first inside page, help the children print the numerals 1–5 in consecutive order. Encourage the children to place the correct number of dinosaur stickers on each corresponding page.

Go on a Dinosaur Egg Hunt

Preparation:

◊ Fill plastic eggs with small toy dinosaurs and/or dinosaur stickers.
◊ Hide the eggs outside or around the classroom.

Give the children small paper bags and invite them to hunt for dinosaur eggs. You may want to ask the children to come back to the group after they find ___ eggs (fill in the number), so all the children have the same opportunity.

What were dinosaurs?

Dinosaur Skeletons

Preparation:

◊ Copy pictures of a few dinosaur skeletons.
◊ Hang the dinosaur skeleton pictures at the children's eye level or place copies on each table.
◊ Set out construction paper, glue, and containers of pasta in various shapes (e.g., spaghetti, linguini, elbows).

Scientists put together fossilized bones to form skeletons so they could learn more about the dinosaurs. Invite the children to make dinosaur skeletons by gluing pasta onto paper. Set aside and allow to dry overnight.

Note: Depending on the shape of the pasta, the children may need to use more glue than usual.

> **Variation:** Mix potting soil and glue with your hands and form it into a ball. Lay the ball on a foam plate and flatten it. Press the pasta into the soil mixture to make a dinosaur skeleton and brush with a fine layer of glue. Set aside and allow to dry overnight. (You should be able to take the "fossils" off the plates after they dry.)

Make Dinosaur Eggs

Preparation:

◊ Blow up balloons and tie them closed. You may want to have a few extra balloons in case some pop.
◊ Set out the balloons, newspapers, and dishes of liquid starch.

Like most reptiles, dinosaur babies hatched from eggs. Invite the children to make their own paper-mâché "dinosaur eggs" by following the steps listed below.

Note: This activity may be more manageable if you work with the children in small groups.

- Tear the newspaper into strips about 1–2 inches wide.
- Dip the torn newspaper strips into the liquid starch and place them on the balloons, smoothing the strips as you go. (Assist the children as needed.)
- Do not layer newspaper at the bottom of the balloon where you tied the balloons closed.
- Add several layers of newspaper to the balloons, letting each layer dry before adding the next.
- Allow the "eggs" to dry overnight. The next day, pop the balloons and pull them out of their paper-mâché shells.
- Invite the children to decorate their dinosaur eggs as desired.

Caution: Always supervise closely when working with balloons. If a balloon should pop, gather all the pieces and discard immediately where the children will not have access to them. Balloon pieces can become a choking hazard if swallowed.

What were dinosaurs?

Dinosaurs Lived Long Ago
(tune: "Twinkle, Twinkle Little Star")

Dinosaurs lived long ago,
They were reptiles, don't you know.
Did you know that some were small,
But most of them were very tall.
Some walked on four legs,
Some on two.
Their babies hatched from eggs, it's true.

Squat down to floor to.
Stand on tiptoes, arms up.
Hold up four fingers.
Touch legs.
Make egg shape with fingers
touching, then open to hatch.

The Dinosaur Song
(tune: "The Wheels on the Bus")

The Tyrannosaurus rex had very sharp teeth,
Very sharp teeth, very sharp teeth.
The Tyrannosaurus rex had very sharp teeth,
A long, long time ago.

Pretend hands are jaws.

The Apatosaurus had a very long neck…

Stretch and slide hand up neck.

The Stegosaurus had plates on its back…

Lean over a bit and tap back.

The Triceratops had three big horns…

Put three fingers on top of head.

Dinosaurs are now extinct,
Now extinct, now extinct.
Dinosaurs are now extinct,
Now there are no more.

Cross hands, as if to say "none."

Dino Pokey
(tune: "Hokey Pokey")

You put your claws in,
You take your claws out,
You put your claws in
And you scratch them all about.
REFRAIN

You put your feet in,
You take your feet out,
You put your feet in
And you stomp them all about.
REFRAIN

You put your teeth in,
You take your teeth out,
You put your teeth in
And you chomp them all about.
REFRAIN

You put your tail in,
You take your tail out,
You put your tail in
And you swing it all about.
REFRAIN

REFRAIN:
You do the dino pokey
And you turn yourself around.
That's what it's all about!

During the first few years of life, children focus their attention on learning about the world around them.

Where does the water go when something dries?
Why does it rain?
What is mud?
What is it like in outer space?

As the children explore the following activities, they will begin to understand the answers to these questions and more!

Earth & Space

What are solids, liquids, and gases?

Building Bridges: Solids, Liquids, and Gases

Preparation:

◊ Gather a cotton ball, wooden block, water bottle with colored water, bowl, and a sealed zipper-top bag with air trapped inside.

◊ Display the items on the floor for all the children to see.

Invite the children to sit in a circle and ask them to name each item. Explain that everything is made up of "stuff" or *matter*. Ask leading questions to help the children explore the displayed items. Is the cotton ball/wooden block hard or soft? How does the "stuff" inside the bottle move? What's inside the bag? Encourage the children to gently explore the items as you discuss each one.

Matter (the "stuff" everything is made of) can be a *solid*, *liquid*, or *gas*. Help the children understand the three states of matter by exploring each of the items as described below.

💡 *Solid – Hold up the cotton ball and wooden block.*

A solid is an object that has a definite shape, but it may or may not be "hard." Cotton balls, feathers, paper, and hair are not hard like the wooden block but are all solids. Some examples of hard solids are bricks, baseballs, and pencils.

💡 *Liquid – Show the water moving inside the bottle. Pass the bottle around so that each child has an opportunity to explore it. After you do this, pour the water into a bowl.*

💡 A liquid takes the shape of the container it's in and flows as you move it. For example, when you pour the water from the bottle into the bowl, it takes the shape of the bowl.

💡 Gas – *Point out the air inside the zipper-top bag.*

A gas is usually invisible and fills the whole container. The air we breathe, the helium in a balloon, and the steam rising from a pot of boiling water are all examples of gases. The matter in a gas zips and zooms everywhere.

💡 Provide the children with visual clues to help them remember the states of matter.
- Point to _____ and say "SOLID" (point to a different object each time).
- Move arms and fingers to make waves and say "LIQUID."
- Breathe out onto palm of hand (to feel the air) and then say "GAS."

The Playdough Challenge:

The next time the children are exploring playdough, ask them to decide if playdough is a solid, liquid, or gas. Although playdough can be squished, it still has shape. Therefore, playdough is a solid!

What are solids, liquids, and gases?

Let's Pretend!

After sharing the following explanations, invite the children to role-play the states of matter as described below. Repeat each action a few times or as long as the children show interest.

Note: Before beginning this activity, you may want to talk to the children about moving safely and making good choices.

- The matter (or "stuff") in a solid is packed tightly together and does not move. Solids have their own shape.
  ACTION: Encourage the children to freeze like statues.

- The matter (or "stuff") in a liquid is spaced a bit apart and moves very slowly. Liquids take the shape of the container they are in.
  ACTION: Encourage the children to stay in a designated area ("container") and move their bodies in a slow, fluid-like way.

- The matter (or "stuff") in a gas is spaced far apart and moves very quickly. Gases fill all the space around us.
  ACTION: Encourage the children to move energetically (but safely) around the whole room.

Play Solid, Liquid, Gas

Invite the children to sit in a circle and choose one child to be It. It should walk around the circle and say "Solid" or "Liquid" as he/she lightly taps each child on the shoulder.

- When It says "Solid" the child who is tapped should freeze like a statue.
- When It says "Liquid" the child who is tapped should move in a slow, fluid-like way (while remaining seated).
- When It says "Gas," the child who is tapped should chase It around the circle and try to tag It before It sits down in the empty spot.

If It is tagged, he/she continues being It. If It sits before being tagged, the other child becomes It.

Solids, Liquids, and Gases

(tune: "London Bridge")

Solids always keep their shape,
Keep their shape, keep their shape.
Solids always keep their shape.
Find a solid!
  *(Children should find and touch
  solids in the room.)*

Liquids always flow and flow,
Flow and flow, flow and flow.
Liquids always flow and flow.
Flow like liquid!
  *(Children should move their
  bodies in a slow fluid-like way.)*

Gases are most everywhere,
Everywhere, everywhere.
Gases are most everywhere.
Move like gases!
  *(Children should move energetically
  around the whole room.)*

What are solids, liquids, and gases?

Build With Blocks

Encourage the children to build structures with blocks and talk about the shapes they see. As the children are exploring, point out how blocks are solids because they have their own shape.

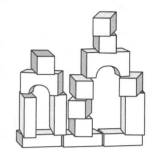

Weigh Solids

Place several different objects on the table. Hold up two items. Have the children predict which of the objects is heavier/lighter. Use a balance scale to test their predictions. Repeat this process, each time comparing two different items.

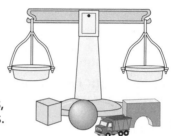

Pour Water

Set out a small plastic pitcher of colored water, several containers in various sizes, and a few funnels. Encourage the children to pour water from one container to the next. As the children are exploring, point out how water is a liquid because it flows and becomes the shape of its container.

Predict and Prove

Show the children one large container and one small container. Have the children predict how many small containers of water it will take to fill the large container. Invite the children to pour water into the large container as you count together. Help the children compare their predictions to the results.

Create Collages

Invite the children to find and cut out pictures of solids and liquids from magazines. Have the children glue the pictures onto large sheets of construction paper and then share what they have found.

Note: This activity focuses on solids and liquids because gases are usually invisible.

What are solids, liquids, and gases?

Caution: Always supervise closely when working with balloons. If a balloon should pop, gather all the pieces and discard immediately where the children will not have access to them. Balloon pieces can become a choking hazard if swallowed.

Building Bridges: Predict and Prove

Preparation:
◊ Bring in one balloon that you blew up and one recently filled with helium.
◊ Tie a long string to each balloon.

Hold the balloons by their strings. Encourage the children to share their ideas about why one balloon falls to the ground but the other rises into the air. Explain that you used two different gases to fill the balloons – air and helium. Since helium is lighter than the air we breathe, it makes the balloon rise into the air.

Blow up another balloon in front of the children and tie it closed. Have the children predict if the balloon will fall to the ground or rise into the air when you let it go. Drop the balloon and help the children compare their predictions to the results.

Play a Balloon Game

Invite the children to stand in a circle. Blow up a balloon and tie it closed. Remind the children that the air inside the balloon is a gas. Tap the balloon into the air and toward the center of the circle. Encourage the children to work together to keep the balloon up in the air.

Variation: Count together to discover how many children tap the balloon before it falls to the ground.

If You're a _____ And You Know It
(tune: "If You're Happy and You Know It")

If you're a solid and you know it keep your shape.
If you're a solid and you know it keep your shape.
If you're a solid and you know it then your shape will surely show it!
If you're a solid and you know it keep your shape.

If you're a liquid and you know it flow and flow.
If you're a liquid and you know it flow and flow.
If you're a liquid and you know it then flow and flow to show it!
If you're a liquid and you know it flow and flow.

If you're a gas and you know it move like air.
If you're a gas and you know it move like air.
If you're a gas and you know it then move like air to show it!
If you're a gas and you know it move like air.

What is ice? What is steam?

Building Bridges: Freeze and Melt

Print each child's name on a 3-ounce bathroom-sized paper cup. Have the children pour water into their cups until they are about half full. Ask the children to determine if the water in their cups is a solid, liquid, or gas, and encourage them to predict what will happen if you put the cups of water into the freezer for a long time. Place the cups on a tray and freeze overnight.

Tom

The next day, give the cups back to the children and invite them to describe what they see and feel. How has the water changed? Is ice a solid, liquid, or gas? Explain that when water gets very, very cold it *freezes* and becomes ice. However, even though the water changed from a liquid to a solid, it is still water. To prove this, place the cups on a windowsill until the ice *melts*. Have the children look in their cups and talk about what they see. Explain that when the temperature of the water gets warmer, ice melts back into a liquid. Either way… it is still water!

Explore Ice

Give each child an ice cube in a sealed zipper-top bag. Invite the children to explore the ice and ask questions to help guide their explorations. What is ice? Is ice a solid, liquid, or gas? How does water freeze into ice? Why does ice melt? As the children are exploring, talk about ice found in nature. Snow, sleet, hail, frost, icicles, and frozen puddles are all forms of ice that can be found in nature.

Note: Depending on where you live, the children may not have personal experiences with ice found in nature.

Paint With Ice

Preparation:

◊ Pour water into ice cube trays (each section should be about ¾ full).

◊ Add red, green, yellow, or blue food coloring to each section until the color becomes very dark. Cover ice cube trays with aluminum foil, insert a craft stick into each section, and freeze overnight.

◊ Cover table(s) with many layers of newspaper or butcher paper and tape in place.

◊ Set out large sheets of white construction paper, paper towels, and the colored ice cubes.

Invite the children to paint with the colored ice cubes by holding onto the craft sticks. As they are painting, encourage the children to notice how the ice begins as a solid and then melts into a liquid. You may want to have the children wear smocks and nonlatex gloves for this activity because food coloring can temporarily stain the skin and permanently stain clothing.

What is ice? What is steam?

Observe Steam

For this activity, you will need a hot pot or access to a stove.

- ☀ Invite the children to sit a safe distance from the pot. Pour water into the pot and explain to the children that you are going to heat it.
- ☀ As the water begins to heat, ask questions to help guide the discussion: Is the water in the pot a solid, liquid, or gas? What do you predict will happen to the water once it gets really hot? How can we tell when it is hot?
- ☀ Once the water boils, explain that the water got so hot it started to boil. Have the children listen to the water boil and describe what they hear.
- ☀ Once the steam rises, explain that when the water gets very, very hot it makes a gas called steam. Although the water changed from a liquid to a gas, it is still water!

Caution: Remind the children to never touch steam or boiling water, and to never go near a stove without an adult.

Ice and Steam

(tune: "Did You Ever See a Lassie?")

Did you ever freeze some water,
Freeze water, freeze water?
Did you ever freeze some water?
It turns into ice!

But it still is water,
Yes it still is water!
Did you ever freeze some water?
It turns into ice!

Did you ever boil some water,
Boil water, boil water?
Did you ever boil some water?
It turns into steam!

But it still is water,
Yes it still is water!
Did you ever boil some water?
It turns into steam!

How much of our earth is water?

Building Bridges: Water Words

Challenge the children to name as many water words as they can and list their words on chart paper. Invite the children to share their experiences with water – swimming in a pool, jumping in puddles, playing in the snow, etc. Some water words are listed below to help you get started:

ocean	river	puddle	rain
sea	stream	pool	snow
lake	brook	ice	wet
pond	creek	steam	liquid

Toss and Catch a Globe

Preparation:

◊ Draw two columns on chart paper.
◊ Print "Water" on the top left and "Land" on the top right.

Invite the children to sit in a circle and show them an inflatable globe. Explain that a *globe* is a model of our planet Earth. The water on this globe is blue and the land is _____ (fill in with an accurate description of your globe). Ask the children to guess if there is more water or land on the earth. To discover the answer, do the following activity.

- Toss the globe around the circle and encourage the children to catch it with two hands.
- As the children catch the globe, they should announce if their thumbs are on water or land.
- Record the results on the chart by drawing blue circles in the left column and green circles in the right column.
- Once all of the children have had a chance to toss and catch the globe, count the circles in each column to discover if there is more water or land on the earth. There should be more blue circles than green circles because the earth is about ¾ water and ¼ land. Note: If partway through the activity you find that your results may be skewed, guide the children to identify the questionable catches as "water."

Taste the "Ocean"

Preparation:

◊ Completely dissolve table salt into a pitcher of warm water until the water has a noticeably salty taste. Refrigerate the water until it is cold.
◊ Pour small samples of the salt water into disposable cups.
◊ Pour small samples of fresh water into disposable cups.

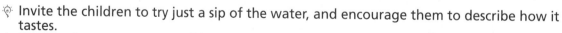

Give each child a cup of salt water, but ask the children to wait to drink it until everyone has been served. (Do not tell them it is salt water.)

- Invite the children to try just a sip of the water, and encourage them to describe how it tastes.
- Explain that we cannot drink most of the water on the earth because it is saltwater. The earth's oceans and seas, as well as some lakes and rivers, are all saltwater bodies.
- Take away these cups and provide each child with a cup of fresh water to drink. Explain that just a small amount of the water on earth is fresh water.

What is the water cycle?

Building Bridges: The Water Cycle

Use the following information to help you explain the water cycle to the children. Draw the water cycle on chart paper and encourage the children to act out each step as it is discussed (e.g., wiggle fingers up in air to symbolize evaporation).

- ☀ A cycle is like a circle – it keeps going around and around. The water on the earth and in the earth's atmosphere goes through a never-ending process called the water cycle.
- ☀ *(Draw water across the bottom of the paper and a sun in the top, left corner.)* When the sun shines, the water on the earth begins to warm.
- ☀ When it gets hot enough, tiny drops of water – so tiny you cannot even see them rise up into the air. *(Draw arrows coming up from the water.)*
- ☀ The higher you go into the air, the cooler it is. As the water in the air begins to cool down, water droplets are formed. These water droplets make a cloud. *(Draw a cloud in the center of the paper.)*
- ☀ When enough water rises up into the air, the cloud gets very heavy. Soon, the water falls back down to earth as rain, snow, sleet, or hail. *(Draw some raindrops, snowflakes, etc. falling into the water.)*
- ☀ Eventually, the sun shines again, heats up the water, and the cycle continues. *(Trace the path of the water cycle by "drawing" a circle with your finger over and over again.)*

Paint the Water Cycle

After you introduce the water cycle, invite the children to paint their own water cycle pictures. As the children are working, encourage them to talk about what they are painting and how the water cycle works.

Sequence the Water Cycle

Preparation:
◊ Make two copies of the "Water Cycle" reproducible (p. 110) for each child.

The water cycle is like a circle because it keeps going around and never stops. Have the children cut out the pictures on both copies of the reproducible and put them in order (sun shines, water evaporates, clouds form, rain falls…). Staple along the edge to make a book. Encourage the children to "read" this story to each other and then to their families at home.

> There is the same amount of water on the earth today as there was when the dinosaurs were alive! This amazing fact is true because of the water *cycle*.

Where does the water go when something dries?

Building Bridges: Evaporation

Give each child a paper towel. Ask the children to determine if their paper towels are wet or dry. Have the children put their paper towels in a bowl of water and squeeze out the excess. Now are the paper towels wet or dry? Why are they wet? Lay the paper towels on a windowsill. Encourage the children to predict what will happen to their paper towels.

A while later, have the children examine their paper towels. The water seems to have disappeared! The water did not really disappear – we just cannot see it anymore. When the sun shines, the water on the earth begins to warm. Eventually, tiny drops of water – so tiny you cannot even see them – rise up into the air.

* *Evaporation* is when water changes from a liquid to a gas, like steam from a pot of boiling water. Once the liquid water evaporates into a gas, it is called *water vapor*.

Conduct an Experiment

Give each child a clear plastic cup with his/her name written on it. Have the children pour water into their cups until they are about half full. Help each child draw a water level line on the outside of the cup with a nontoxic permanent marker, then place the cups on a windowsill. Over the next few days, examine the cups of water together. The children will likely notice that the water level is lower each day. Reinforce the concept of evaporation after the children examine their cups each day.

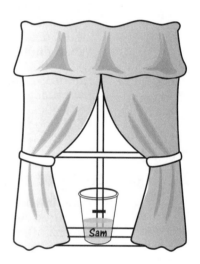

> **Variation:** In addition to the children's cups, prepare another cup of water and cover it tightly with plastic wrap. Over time, the children should be able to see the evaporated water condense on the plastic wrap. Point out how the level of water doesn't change as much (or not all), because the plastic traps the water before it can evaporate into the air. Eventually the water on the plastic wrap falls back into the cup like rain.

Paint With Water

Invite the children to "paint" on a chalkboard or the pavement with water. Encourage them to watch closely as the water evaporates. Is it magic? No! It is evaporation! Continue painting with water as long as the children show interest.

Earth & Space

Building Bridges: Clouds

When the weather permits, invite the children to lie down on blankets and observe the clouds. Are the clouds thick and fluffy, or thin and wispy? Do any of the clouds look like animals or other figures?

The higher you go into the air, the cooler it is. As the water in the air begins to cool down, water droplets are formed. These water droplets come together to make a cloud.

* *Condensation* is when the water vapor in the air cools and turns back from a gas to a liquid. We can see condensation in the form of clouds or on the outside of a cold drink on a hot day.

Note: You may want to share information about some types of clouds, as well.

- Cirrus (SEER-us) – high, wispy clouds
- Cumulonimbus (CUE-mue-lo-**NIM**-bus) – dark storm clouds
- Cumulus (CUE-mue-lus) – white, fluffy clouds
- Stratus (STRA-tus) – low white or gray clouds that look like a thick blanket

Cotton Ball Clouds

Invite children to glue cotton balls onto blue construction paper to make clouds. Encourage them to stretch, squish, or reshape the cotton balls to make different types of clouds.

Paint With "Clouds"

Give each child a large sheet of blue construction paper and a cotton ball. Encourage the children to pretend that their cotton balls are clouds. Invite the children to dip their "clouds" in white paint and press them on the paper to make cloud prints. Display the children's artwork after the paintings have dried.

Play What Time Is It Mr. Cloud?

Have the children stand shoulder to shoulder with some space between them. Stand about 30 feet away on a line parallel with the children. The children should ask, "What time is it Mr. Cloud?" Mr. Cloud should then respond, "It is ___ o'clock" (fill in the hour). For every hour that is given, the children take that many steps toward Mr. Cloud. Repeat until all of the children have reached the line on which you are standing. Each time you play, invite a different child to be the Cloud.

Note: Substitute Miss, Mrs., or Ms. for Mr. as appropriate.

Why does it rain?

Building Bridges: Rain

Give each child a cotton ball and a shallow bowl of cold water. Encourage the children to pretend the cotton ball is a cloud and the bowl of water is a lake. Ask the children if their "clouds" are light or heavy.

Have the children hold the cotton balls on the surface of the water. As the cotton balls soak up the water, tell them to imagine that tiny drops of water – so tiny you can't even see them – are rising up into the air, cooling down, and forming a cloud. Once the cotton balls are saturated with water, have the children lift them above the bowls to see it rain. Ask leading questions to help guide the children's observations: What is happening now? Does the cloud feel light or heavy? Does it feel cold or warm? Explain that when enough water rises into the air, the clouds get very heavy. Soon, the water falls back down to earth as rain, snow, sleet, or hail.

* This step of the water cycle is called *precipitation*. Below are the four main forms of precipitation:

- Rain – water that falls to earth in the form of liquid
- Snow – water that falls to earth in the form of ice crystals; each snowflake has six sides
- Sleet – snow that partially melts before it hits the ground, but not enough to be called rain
- Hail – balls or clumps of ice that are formed from storm clouds (cumulonimbus clouds)

Sound Like Rain

Invite the children to use their bodies to sound like rain. Have the children sit in a circle with their knees bent and their feet on the floor. (In this activity, the teacher is the leader.) Begin by rubbing the palms of your hands together to sound like it's sprinkling. Going around the circle, each child repeats the motion and continues to do it until the leader changes it. Perform each action as described below.

- Sprinkling Rain – *Rub palms of hands together.*
- Light Rain – *Snap fingers.*
- Heavy Rain – *Quickly tap hands on thighs.*
- Thunder – *Quickly stomp with feet.*

(To end the storm, repeat the steps in reverse order.)

Why does it rain?

Fingerprint Raindrops

Set out white or light blue paper, blue washable-ink pads, and other art materials. Invite the children to make fingerprints on the paper to represent raindrops. They may also want to decorate their rainy pictures in other ways using additional art materials.

Rain, Rain, Go Away

(traditional tune)

Rain, rain, go away!
Come again another day.
We want to go outside and play.
Rain, rain, go away!

Play a Rain Game

Invite the children to sit in a circle. Have the children gently pass a blue beanbag around the circle as you sing "Rain, Rain, Go Away." Once the song is over, the child left holding the beanbag should stand up, point to the sky and say, "It's still raining!", then sit back down. Continue to play as long as the children show interest.

Jump In and Over Puddles

Cut ten puddle shapes out of blue construction paper and number them from 1–10. Securely attach the puddles to the floor in consecutive order with clear tape, leaving about two feet between each puddle. Ask the children to explain what a puddle is. (Rain that has collected on the ground.) Invite the children to jump "in the puddles" as they count from 1–10. Once everyone has had a turn, have the children jump "over the puddles," counting as they go.

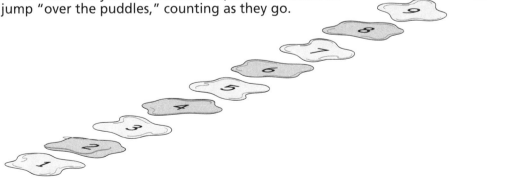

What is snow?

Building Bridges: Snow

Ask the children to explain why it rains. (Water in the air rises, cools, gets too heavy, and falls back to the earth.) What makes it snow? (Colder temperatures freeze the water droplets into snowflake crystals.) Depending upon where you live, the children may not have personal experiences with snow. If that is the case, you may want to show a video clip of falling snow. Encourage the children to describe what they see and imagine how snow might feel.

Make a Mural

Hang a large sheet of blue butcher paper at the children's eye level. Set out sponges, white paint, and other white art materials (e.g., small bars of soap, doilies, pom-poms, paper, yarn, chalk). Invite the children to design a snowy scene using the materials. They could draw with the soap, glue on doilies, or dip sponges in white paint and press onto the paper.

> **Variation:** If you do not have blue butcher paper, you could have the children design their own snowy scenes on large sheets of blue construction paper.

Toss and Catch Snowballs

Have the children make "snowballs" by crumpling white paper. Invite the children to toss the snowballs in the air and catch them.

> **Variation:** Divide the children into groups of three or four. Have each group stand in a circle and gently toss a snowball to each other.

What is snow?

Make Snowflake Bracelets

Preparation:
◊ Cut chenille stems into 10-inch segments.
◊ Set out clear, white, and silver tri-shape beads.

Invite the children to thread the chenille stems through the beads, then help them twist the ends together to make bracelets.

Note: You may want to show the children photographs of snowflakes to remind them that real snowflakes have six points, not three.

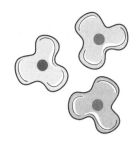

Snowflakes
(tune: "London Bridge")

Dance like snowflakes in the air –
Whirling, twirling everywhere.
Softly falling to the ground –
Snowflakes, snowflakes all around.

Let's Pretend!

Invite the children to move like snowflakes. They could gently fall to the ground or whirl and twirl in the wind. Play soft music in the background as your little snowflakes dance around the classroom.

What is temperature?

Building Bridges: Temperature

Preparation:

◊ Draw a large thermometer on posterboard and label it in 10° increments from 0° to 100°.
◊ Attach pieces of Velcro (hook side) at each temperature mark.
◊ Cut a long piece of red felt to fit inside your thermometer.
◊ Display the thermometer at the children's eye level.

Show the children a digital thermometer and a standard thermometer. Ask the children if they ever have had their temperature taken when they were sick. Explain that both items are called *thermometers* and are used to find the temperature inside their bodies.

Explain to the children that thermometers can also be used to find the temperature of the air. The air around us could be hot, warm, cool, or cold. The warmth or coolness of the air is also called the *temperature*, which we measure with a thermometer. If it's a hot day, it might be 90° (move red felt to the 90° mark). A warm day might be 70° (move felt to the 70° mark). If it's a cool day, it might be 50° (move felt to the 50° mark). A cold day might be 30° (move felt to the 30° mark). Take the children outside and talk about the temperature for that day.

Note: If the children demonstrate readiness, point out how even though the temperature markings skip count by tens, the temperature could be anywhere between two marks.

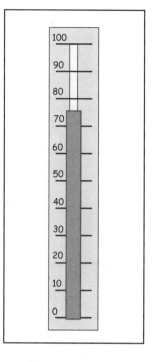

Walk Along a Thermometer

Preparation:

◊ Draw a very large thermometer on the sidewalk.
◊ Space the temperature marks evenly with at least two feet between each one.
◊ Label the thermometer in 10° increments from 0° to 100°.

As you point to each temperature mark, skip count by tens and encourage the children to join in! Have the children line up at the 0° mark. Invite them to take turns walking along the thermometer as you count by tens together.

Variation: If you need to do this activity indoors, draw the thermometer on a large sheet of butcher paper and securely attach the paper to the floor with clear tape.

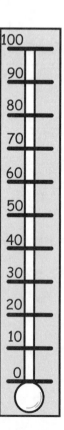

What is temperature?

Hot, Warm, Cool, Cold

Cold days with snow and ice,
Warm days are very nice!
Hot days I'm in the pool,
It's lots of fun and very cool!

Note: Talk about the two meanings of
the word *cool*. Point out how the word
cool in this rhyme can actually have either
meaning.

Play Hot and Cold

Choose two children to be the Detectives and ask
them to close their eyes. Secretly hide a familiar
object in the classroom as the rest of the children
watch. (Make sure the object is one-of-a-kind
and that all the children know what it looks like.)
When the Detectives turn around, they must
stay together and try to find the hidden object.
As the Detectives walk around the room, the
other children should help the Detectives find
the missing object by saying "hot" when they
are moving toward it and "cold" when they are
moving away from it. Repeat the game, each
time choosing different Detectives.

Create Collages

Invite the children to tear or cut out pictures of hot
and cold things (and/or activities you do on hot and
cold days) from magazines and glue the pictures onto
construction paper. As the children are working, invite
the children to talk about the pictures they find.

What is the weather like today?

Building Bridges: Weather

Preparation:
- ◊ Draw and cut out large pictures of the following: sun, cloud, raindrop, and snowflake.
- ◊ Display the weather symbols at the children's eye level.

Each day, take the children outside or have them look out a nearby window. Invite the children to describe the weather based on their observations. Have the children determine which weather description and symbol best fits the day – sunny, mostly cloudy (but dry), rainy, or snowy.

Walk Along a Thermometer

Preparation:
- ◊ Staple several sheets of plain white paper between two sheets of colored cardstock or construction paper. Include at least one page for each child in your class.
- ◊ Print "Our Weather Journal" on the front.

After discussing the weather each day, choose one child to draw a picture of the weather for that day in the weather journal. Print the child's name, date, and the child's description of the weather (exactly as he/she describes it), as well. Continue this activity until all the children have had an opportunity to record the weather at least once.

Our Weather Journal

Graph the Weather

Preparation:
- ◊ Draw four columns on chart paper.
- ◊ Draw the following weather symbols across the bottom of the chart with one symbol in each column: sun, cloud, raindrop, and snowflake.

After discussing the weather each day, choose a child to put a red coding dot (on hot or warm days) or a blue coding dot (on cold or cool days) in the appropriate column. At the end of the week, count the coding dots to determine which weather pattern occurred the most frequently and which occurred the least.

What's the Weather Like Today?

(tune: "London Bridge")

What's the weather like today?
Bright and sunny,
Cloudy and gray?
Will it rain or will it snow?
I would really like to know!

What is the weather like today?

Predict the Weather

Many people plan their upcoming activities based on weather predictions. When we make a "prediction" it's often a guess, but a weather prediction is based on a lot of scientific information. *Meteorologists* are scientists who study the weather and predict what the weather will be over the next few days.

Take the children outside or have them look out a nearby window. Invite the children to describe the weather based on their observations, then predict what they think the weather might be like tomorrow. Record the children's predictions on chart paper next to their names. The next day, check the weather with the children to see if their predictions were correct.

Sort Clothes

Preparation:
◊ Bring in a variety of clothing and other items to represent each major weather pattern.
◊ Some examples are: swimsuits, flip-flops, shorts, umbrellas, rain boots, raincoats, snowsuits, mittens, and scarves .
◊ Set out three laundry baskets and label as follows: Hot and Sunny (draw sun), Rainy (draw rain coming from cloud), Cold and Snowy (draw "wind" and snow).

Place all the clothing and other items on a table or the floor. Hold up each piece and have the children name what it is. Point out the laundry baskets and read the weather words on each basket. Invite the children to sort the clothing/items into the appropriate baskets.

Play Sunny Day, Rainy Day

Invite the children to sit in a circle. As you play recorded music, the children should gently but quickly pass a yellow beanbag (sun) and a blue beanbag (rain) around the circle. When you stop the music, the child left holding the "sun" and "rain" should run around the circle and sit back in their own spots. When you restart the music, the children should pass the beanbags again.

Note: Start the game with the beanbags on opposite sides of the circle, and have the children pass the beanbags in the same direction.

What are rocks? What is sand?

Building Bridges: Go on a Rock Hunt

Take the children outside and go on a rock hunt. Encourage the children to find rocks in a variety of sizes, shapes, and colors. Invite each child to show his/her favorite rock to the rest of the class.

Note: You may want to wash the rocks in a bucket of water before bringing them inside.

Explore Rocks

Set out several different rocks that you and the children have collected. Have the children work together to sort the rocks, but do not instruct them on how the rocks should be sorted at first. After exploring a few ideas, make suggestions about how to sort them (e.g., shape, size, weight, texture, color).

Invite each child to choose a rock from the pile to explore. Using magnifying glasses and their senses, encourage the children to examine their rocks and share their discoveries. As the children explore, ask engaging questions such as: What color is your rock? What shape is it? Is your rock smooth or bumpy? Is it light or heavy?

Weigh Rocks

Set out five or six rocks. (Try to choose rocks that are deceivingly light or heavy in comparison to their size.) Hold up two of the rocks. Have the children predict which of the two rocks is heavier/lighter. Use a balance scale to test their predictions. Repeat this process several times, each time weighing a different pair of rocks.

Play Geologist, Geologist, Where's Your Rock?

Geologists are scientists who search for and study rocks. Invite the children to pretend they are geologists as they play the game described below. Continue to play until all of the children have had an opportunity to be the Geologist.

- One child should sit on a chair with his/her eyes closed, facing away from the rest of class. (This child is the Geologist.) Place a medium-sized rock undere the chair.
- Have the other children sit side by side on the floor 15-20 feet behind the Geologist.
- Secretly choose one child to walk up to the Geologist's chair, take the rock, then sit back down and hide the rock.
- The children on the floor should put their hands in their laps, as if they were all hiding the rock, then say, "Geologist, geologist, where's your rock?"
- The Geologist should turn around and try to determine who has taken the rock. Give the child three guesses. Reveal who took the rock if the Geologist does not guess correctly.
- Invite the child who took the rock to be the Geologist, and play again!

What are rocks? What is sand?

Paint With Rocks

Preparation:
◊ Gather coffee cans with lids, plain white paper, tempera paint, small rocks, and plastic spoons.
◊ Cut the paper to fit along the inside of a coffee can without overlapping or sticking out the top.

Invite the children to create abstract paintings using rocks! This can be a messy (and loud) activity, so you will want to plan accordingly. Have the children follow these steps to paint with rocks:

- Place a piece of paper along the inside of a coffee can.
- Gently drop a rock into a bowl of paint. Using a plastic spoon, remove the rock from the paint and place it in the can. (Try not to pour any excess paint in the can along with the rock.)
- Put the lid on the coffee can. Shake and roll the can to move the rock around inside.
- Remove the rock from the can and place it back into the paint.
- Repeat these steps with two or three more colors of paint, each time using a different rock.
- Carefully remove the paper from the coffee can and set it aside to dry.

Explore Sand

Give each child a bowl of sand. Using magnifying glasses and their senses, encourage the children to examine the sand. What does it look like? What does it feel like? Explain that sand is actually rocks and/or seashells that have broken down into very tiny pieces. Set out funnels, plastic cups, toy shovels and spoons, and invite the children to explore the sand further.

Caution: Remind the children about safety when exploring sand (e.g., don't throw, don't rub eyes). Supervise closely as the children play.

Design Sand Art

Give each child a sanitized, pint-sized water bottle and a funnel. Set out bowls of colored sand and invite the children to create designs with the sand by layering different colors in the bottle. After each child has finished, pour a light layer of glue on the top layer of sand and set aside to dry overnight. Once dry, replace the cap.

Note: This activity may be more manageable if you work with small groups.

I've Got a Rock
(tune: "My Bonnie Lies Over the Ocean")

I've got a rock here in my pocket.
It's smooth and it's shiny and round.
I've got a rock here in my pocket.
I found my rock on the ground.

I've got some sand here in my bucket.
But sand is just tiny rocks.
I've got some sand here in my bucket.
I'll pour it into my sandbox.

What is dirt (soil)? What is mud?

Building Bridges: Digging in Dirt

Give each child a disposable cup and a sturdy spoon. Invite the children to go outside and dig in the dirt. Challenge the children to find more than one kind of dirt (e.g., some soil is sandy, some is sticky like clay). Explain that dirt (or soil) is made up of tiny pieces of rock and dead plant material. Using magnifying glasses and their senses, encourage the children to examine the soil. Have the children describe what they see and feel.

Compare Soil Samples

Give each child a cup of untreated potting soil. Have the children compare the potting soil with soil samples collected outside. As the children explore, ask questions to help guide their observations. In what ways are the soil samples the same? How are they different?

Explore Mud

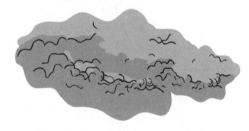

Although mud is made of just dirt and water, it can be very useful. For example, some people make houses out of mud bricks, pigs roll in the mud to stay cool, and some animals make their homes in muddy places. Set out bowls of dirt, small cups of water, and plastic spoons. Encourage the children to experiment with the dirt and water. What happens when you put just a few drops of water in the dirt? What happens when you add more water? Is mud wet or dry? Set a bowl of mud outside in the sun on a hot day. What happened to the mud? How did that happen?

Variations:
(1) Provide paper to those children who wish to finger paint with mud.
(2) Set out small toy trucks and plastic animals with which the children can make mud tracks.

Mud

Mud is brown. Mud is sticky.
Mud is wet. Mud is icky.
Mud is useful. Mud is fun.
Mud becomes dirt
In the hot, hot sun.

What is a cave? What is a volcano?

Building Bridges: Caves and Volcanoes

Show the children photographs of caves and volcanoes. Encourage the children to describe what they see or share what they know about caves and volcanoes. Use the following information to help facilitate the discussion:

- ☼ Caves and volcanoes are made by nature.
- ☼ Caves are formed as water crashes and eventually runs through the rocky land. Over many years, stalactites and stalagmites are formed by water leaving behind tiny deposits of calcium carbonate as it drips from the ceiling to the ground. *Stalactites* are the icicle-shaped rocks that hang down from the ceiling, while *stalagmites* are the icicle-shaped rocks that grow upward from the ground. (You can use the "c" in stalactite to remember ceiling, and the "g" in stalagmite to remember ground.)
- ☼ Volcanoes are large, often cone-shaped landforms created when magma (molten rock far beneath the earth's surface) pushes its way through a vent on the earth's surface called a crater. Once the magma comes in contact with air it is called lava. Over time, the lava cools and becomes a new layer on the earth.

Make "Cave Paintings"

Preparation:

- ◊ Cut the sides of brown paper grocery bags in uneven shapes.
- ◊ Set out the paper bag sections and markers (red, yellow, brown, black).

Caves are natural shelters. Thousands of years ago, people lived in caves to protect themselves from bad weather and wild animals. But how do we know that people lived there if it was so long ago? These cave dwellers used crushed rocks, burned wood, or even soil and leaves to "paint" pictures on the walls. The paintings were often of animals, such as wild horses, bison, deer, and rabbits.

Share some information about cave paintings with the children, then invite them to create their very own "cave art." Have each child take one paper bag section and crumple it into a ball. Show the children how to lay the paper bag flat and smooth it out a bit. Encourage the children to draw pictures on their "cave walls" using red, yellow, brown, and black markers. Explain that these colors were used to create the first cave paintings made thousands of years ago.

Erupt a "Volcano"

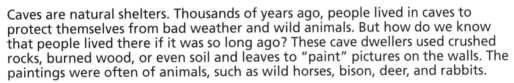

Preparation:

- ◊ Gather an aluminum pan, clay, plastic medicine cup, baking soda, red food coloring, white vinegar, and an eyedropper.
- ◊ Anchor the medicine cup to the pan with a small amount of clay.

Invite the children to mold a "volcano" around the medicine cup with clay. After the volcano is formed, fill the cup with baking soda about halfway and add one or two drops of red food coloring. Next, have each child squeeze a few drops of vinegar into the cup using an eyedropper. The baking soda and vinegar will create a chemical reaction causing the "volcano to erupt."

Note: You can add more baking soda if necessary.

What is pollution?

Building Bridges: Pollution

Pollution can be found almost everywhere on our earth – on land, in water, even in the air! Trash on the ground, oil spills in the ocean, and exhaust from cars are just a few types of pollution. Pollution is anything that ruins our earth or harms living things. Help the children brainstorm ways they can help protect our earth and list their ideas on chart paper.

Clean Dirty Water

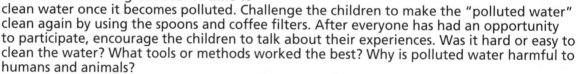

Preparation:

◊ Cover table(s) with many layers of newspapers or butcher paper and tape in place.
◊ In a large aluminum pan with high sides, mix dirt, cooking oil, and pieces of torn paper into colored water.
◊ Set out the "polluted water," two empty pans, a few plastic spoons, and several coffee filters.

Polluted water is very hard to clean. It takes a lot of work and a great deal of time to clean water once it becomes polluted. Challenge the children to make the "polluted water" clean again by using the spoons and coffee filters. After everyone has had an opportunity to participate, encourage the children to talk about their experiences. Was it hard or easy to clean the water? What tools or methods worked the best? Why is polluted water harmful to humans and animals?

Note: This activity may be more manageable in small groups.

Go on a "Trash" Walk

Preparation:

◊ Crumple several sheets of newspaper and scatter the newspaper "trash" around the room.
◊ Set out a new or sanitized trash can in the center of the room.

Take the children on a trash walk around the classroom. Encourage the children to work together to clean up any "trash" they find on the ground. Remind the children that trash belongs in a trash can, not on the ground.

How can we help save the earth?

Building Bridges: Reduce, Reuse, Recycle

There are three things we can all do to help save the earth:

- We can reduce the amount of trash we produce and the amount of natural resources we use, such as water and energy. By simply turning off the water when we brush our teeth or shutting off lights in rooms when we aren't using them, we can begin to preserve our natural resources!
- We can reuse items instead of always getting new ones. For example, save your plastic grocery bags and use them again the next time you go shopping, or refill water bottles instead of buying new ones.
- We can recycle many materials. Recycling is when something that cannot be reused anymore goes through a process to make it useful again. Newspapers, glass, and soda cans are just a few items that can be recycled.

Help the children brainstorm ways they can reduce, reuse, and recycle, and list their ideas on chart paper. Divide the class into three groups and cheer together: "Reduce! Reuse! Recycle!" (each group shouts one word).

From Trash to Treasure

For a week or two before this activity, ask the children and their families to save (and sanitize when applicable) any non-perishable trash, such as soda bottles, plastic jugs, yogurt cups, cereal boxes, and newspapers. Set out the "trash" and a variety of art materials. Invite the children to turn the trash into creative pieces of artwork.

Reduce, Reuse, Recycle

(tune: "Yankee Doodle")

Reduce, reuse, recycle now
To save our lovely planet.
The earth's our home
And we should do
All we can to protect it.

What can be found in outer space?

Building Bridges: Our Solar System

Our *solar system* is a group of planets that revolve (orbit) around our closest star – the sun. Show the children a photograph of Earth as seen from space, and encourage them to share what they know about our planet as a part of the solar system. Use the following information to help facilitate the discussion:

- There are eight planets in our solar system: Mercury, Venus, Earth, Mars, Jupiter, Saturn, Uranus, and Neptune. (Confused? See the box at the bottom of the page.) Earth is the third planet from the sun.
- It takes one year (365 days, or 366 every leap year) for the Earth to revolve around the sun.
- The angle of the Earth as it orbits the sun is what causes the seasons. For example, when it is winter in the northern hemisphere, it is summer in the southern hemisphere. The land around the equator, however, always receives the most direct sunlight and therefore is hot year-round.
- It takes 24 hours for the Earth to rotate on its axis. This rotation is what causes day and night.

Make the Sun

Preparation:
- Cut yellow and orange streamers into several strips about 12 inches long.
- Set out large paper plates, the streamers, and a variety of art materials.

Have the children tear and glue small pieces of paper onto paper plates or paint them. Once the children have decorated their plates, they may want to glue or tape streamers around the plates to look like the sun's rays.

Create Star Collages

The sun is our closest star, but what is a star? A star is a mass of gases held together by its own gravity. Invite the children to make collages by placing star stickers on black construction paper.

Note: Remind the children that real stars aren't shaped like the star stickers they are using to make their collages.

Since 1930, Pluto was considered to be the ninth planet in our solar system. However, in August 2006, members of the International Astronomical Union decided that Pluto did not fit the criteria to be considered a true planet.

What can be found in outer space?

Explore Gravity

Gravity is the force or pull toward something. The sun's gravity keeps the planets from drifting off into outer space. The Earth's gravity keeps the moon orbiting our planet and causes things that go up to come back down. Encourage the children to explore gravity in two easy ways:

- Safely toss objects up into the air and watch them fall back to the earth.
- Hold your arms out to the sides until they feel heavy. By doing so, you are working against the pull of gravity. That's why your arms get tired!

Let's Pretend!

Encourage the children to squat down to the floor. Count down with the children from 10–1. Shout "Blast off!" together and jump up into the air! Invite the children to describe what they "see" on their space adventure. This is an excellent way to review the planets and other features of our solar system.

Variation: Neil Armstrong was the first human to have ever walked on the moon. His footprints, and the footprints of the other astronauts, are still intact because there is no wind on the moon to blow the footprints away. The moon also has a much lower force of gravity (or downward pull) than the Earth, so making long leaps across the surface of the moon is easy to do. Invite the children to pretend they are walking on the moon.

Toss and Catch Meteorites

Meteorites are pieces of rock from space that have entered our Earth's atmosphere, ranging in size from a grain of sand to a boulder. Have the children make "meteorites" by crumpling large sheets of aluminum foil. Invite the children to toss the meteorites in the air and catch them.

Variation: Divide the children into groups of three or four. Have each group stand in a circle and gently toss a meteorite to each other.

Shadows, rainbows, magnets, and more are especially intriguing to children, yet learning about physical science is often overlooked in the early childhood classroom. By providing several opportunities for hands-on exploration, even young children may begin to discover the many wonders of the physical world!

Exploration Station

How are rainbows made?

Building Bridges: Rainbows

Light is a combination of all the colors in the spectrum. Rainbows can be seen when tiny water droplets or a prism separates light into its distinct colors. Obviously, the best way to explore rainbows is to see a real one, but you cannot anticipate when a natural rainbow will occur. Instead of waiting for a sun shower, make your own rainbow using one of the two ways described below:

- Invite the children to join you outside on a sunny day. Have small groups of children stand with their backs toward the sun and spray a fine mist of water in front of them (preferably from a garden hose). The children should be able to see a rainbow in the mist.
- Bring a crystal prism into the classroom. Hold the prism in a ray of sunlight and a beautiful rainbow should appear!

Move With Rainbow Ribbons

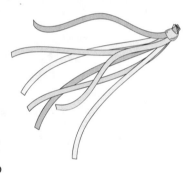

Preparation:
- ◊ Cut many colors of ribbon or streamers into 3-foot long segments.
- ◊ Tie the ribbons/streamers together on one end. Be sure each cluster has multiple colors.

Invite the children to name the colors in their rainbow ribbons. Encourage the children to move in various ways with their ribbons. They could fly their ribbons high in the air, make circles, or pretend they are butterflies fluttering from flower to flower. Play recorded music in the background and invite the children to move to the music with their rainbow ribbons.

I'm a Little Rainbow
(tune: "I'm a Little Teapot")

I'm a little rainbow
In the sky.
See my pretty colors
Way up high!
When the sun shines
And the rain falls down,
Then a rainbow can be found!

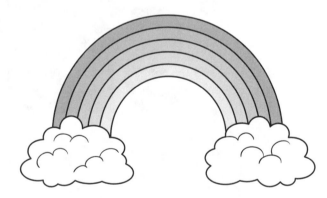

How are rainbows made?

Sort a Rainbow

Preparation:
◊ Draw or cut out pictures of several fruits and vegetables.
◊ Attach each picture to a separate index card. (You may also want to laminate the cards or cover with contact paper.)

Fruits and vegetables have many vitamins and minerals that we need to stay healthy, and give us energy so we can work and play. We should "eat a rainbow" of at least five fruits and vegetables every day! Encourage the children to sort the pictures of fruits and vegetables by color. (See examples listed below.)

- Red – strawberries, red apples, tomatoes
- Orange – carrots, oranges, sweet potatoes
- Yellow – corn, pineapple, yellow peppers
- Green – broccoli, celery, green grapes
- Blue/Purple – blueberries, plums, purple cabbage

Eat a Rainbow

Preparation:
◊ Cut paper plates in half to form a rainbow shape.
◊ Set out bowls of fruity oat-ring cereal.

Invite the children to make rainbows with fruity oat-ring cereal. Display a picture of a rainbow and encourage the children to put the colors on their plates in "rainbow order" – red, orange, yellow, green, (blue), purple. After the children have created their rainbows, they may eat their colorful artwork!

Note: If you cereal does not contain blue oat rings, you could use blueberries instead.

Mix Finger Paint

The three primary colors are red, yellow, and blue. These colors can be combined to form the three secondary colors: red + yellow = orange, yellow + blue = green, and blue + red = purple.

Set out red, yellow, blue, and white finger paints. Invite the children to mix the colors on finger-paint paper to form new colors. Have the children experiment by adding more of one primary color and/or small amounts of white to darken or lighten a color. As the children explore, encourage them to talk about their color discoveries.

What are shadows?
What are reflections?

Building Bridges: Search for Shadows

Take the children outside on a sunny day. Encourage the children to find shadows (other than their own) and determine what object is casting each shadow. Explain that shadows are made when the sun or other light shines behind an object.

Shadow Dance

Invite the children to dance around and watch their shadows dance along with them! You may want to play music in the background as the children shadow dance.

My Shadow

On bright and sunny days,
My shadow, do I see.
When I run and jump and play
It does the same as me.

We go everywhere together,
We have lots and lots of fun.
I love to see my shadow
When I play out in the sun.

Make Shadow Puppets

Shine a powerful flashlight or overhead projector on the wall. Invite the children to make shadow puppets with their hands. For example, open and close your fingers to make a quacking duck, or cross your thumbs and watch a majestic eagle fly away.

What are shadows?
What are reflections?

See Shadow Shapes

Cut shapes from the center of 5" x 8" index cards. Shine a flashlight through the hole on each card to illuminate the shape on the wall. Encourage the children to identify each shining shape and describe its characteristics, such as a triangle has three sides.

> **Variation:** Cut shapes from 5" x 8" index cards and attach to craft sticks. Shine a flashlight behind each shape to see the shadow of the shape on the wall. Encourage the children to identify each shadow shape and describe its characteristics, such as a square has four sides that are the same.

Play Shadow Tag

Divide the children into pairs and show them how to "tag" the other person by jumping on his/her shadow. Once the child who is It "catches" his/her partner's shadow, the children switch roles.

Search for Reflections

Ask the children to explain what a reflection is and where they might see a reflection. Walk around the classroom and take the children outside to find reflections. Look for reflections in mirrors, windows, and even puddles on the ground.

Explore Reflections

Use aluminum foil taped to posterboard (shiny side out) or unbreakable hand mirrors to experiment with light and reflections. Provide several opportunities for the children to experiment with light and reflections, and watch your young scientists at work! As the children are exploring, encourage them to predict where the light will reflect or challenge them to reflect the light in a specified area.

How do I know air is there?

Building Bridges: Invisible Air

Air is all around us. We cannot see air, but we can feel it, hear it, and see its effects. Encourage the children to talk about their "air experiences." Some children may describe the light breeze at the beach, while others may tell about strong winds on a stormy day. Set out old bedsheets, a parachute, and/or plastic bags. Challenge the children to "catch air" using the materials.

Caution: Put the plastic bags away when finished with the activity.

Conduct an Experiment

Remind the children that gravity is the pull that causes objects to fall back down to the earth. Give each child two sheets of paper that are the same size, and ask the children to crumple the paper into balls. Have the children hold the two crumpled balls of paper, one in each hand, in front of their bodies. Encourage the children to predict what will happen when they drop the papers at the same time, then test their predictions. Repeat several times. Now have the children open and flatten one sheet of paper. Again, have the children hold the crumpled paper in one hand and the flattened sheet in the other in front of their bodies, predict what will happen, then drop the papers at the same time. What happened? The flattened sheet of paper should have taken longer to land on the ground. Why did that happen? The flattened paper "catches" the air, which causes it to fall more slowly.

Paint With Air

Preparation:

◊ Cover table(s) with many layers of newspapers or butcher paper and tape in place.
◊ Cut a small slit in the middle of a long plastic straw for each child. (Do not use flexible straws.)
◊ Set out bowls of slightly watered-down tempera paint and plastic spoons.

Give each child a straw and a large sheet of white construction paper. Have the children place one spoonful of paint on their papers at a time. Encourage the children to create designs on their papers by blowing the paint with air through a straw.

Let's Pretend!

Encourage the children to look outside on a partly cloudy day. Do the clouds stay in one spot or do they move? What causes them to move? Scatter cotton balls on a table or the floor. Invite the children to pretend to be wind by blowing the "clouds" away.

Are all bubbles round?

Building Bridges: Blow Bubbles

Take the children outside for some bubble fun! Provide bottles or trays of bubble solution and a variety of bubble blowing tools. Encourage the children to watch the bubbles float away and eventually pop. Depending upon the bubble solution that you use, the children may be able to see a rainbow swirling around each bubble!

Paint With Bubbles

Preparation:
◊ Cover table(s) with many layers of newspapers or butcher paper and tape in place.
◊ Cut a small slit in the middle of a long plastic straw for each child. (Do not use flexible straws.)
◊ Mix 2 tablespoons tempera paint, 4 tablespoons liquid dish soap, and ½ cup water to create a colorful bubble solution.

Give each child a straw, sheet of plain white paper, and a small bowl of the bubble solution. Point out that when the children hold the straw, they should not cover the slit. (This is a precautionary measure to lower the chances of the children sucking up the bubble solution.) Give each child a small bowl of bubble solution. Encourage the children to blow bubbles with the straw until the bubbles form a mound above the bowl's rim. Before the bubbles begin to pop, show the children how to gently place their papers on top of the bubbles. When they remove the paper, the children should see a colorful design formed by the popping bubbles. If the children want to paint with more than one color, provide them with another bowl of bubble solution and a new straw.

Note: Be cautious that the children do not share straws to eliminate the spread of germs.

Conduct an Experiment

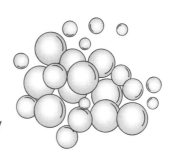

Are all bubbles round? Encourage the children to share their predictions, then conduct the following experiment to answer the question. Show the children how to use long chenille stems to make their own bubble wands in many different shapes – triangles, squares, even squiggles (any shape is fine as long as it is closed and twisted onto the stem). Invite the children to blow bubbles with the wands that they made. The children may be surprised to find that all bubbles are round, regardless of the wand shape!

Toss and Catch "Bubbles"

Blow up several punching balls and tie them. Ask the children to imagine that the punching balls are bubbles. Invite the children to toss and catch the "bubbles" in small groups.

What objects sink?
What objects float?

Building Bridges: Make Clay Float

Ask the children to explain what it means to sink and float. Provide each child with a container of water and a lump of clay about the size of a golf ball. Encourage the children to predict if the clay will sink or float then test their predictions. (The clay will sink.) Challenge the children to reshape the clay so it will float on the surface of the water. Invite the children to share their discoveries with their classmates after each child has had sufficient time to experiment with the clay.

Predict and Prove

Set out a variety of small objects and a deep pan of water. Encourage the children to sort the items into two groups – those that will sink and those that will float. After all the items have been sorted, have the children test their predictions.

Build a Better Boat

Set out several sheets of aluminum foil in many different sizes. Invite the children to build "boats" with the foil so they will float on the water. After each child creates a boat that floats, he/she should gently place pennies in their boats one at a time. Have the children count how many pennies their boats held before they began to sink. Challenge the children to build better boats that can hold even more pennies! (Try it! It's harder than you think!)

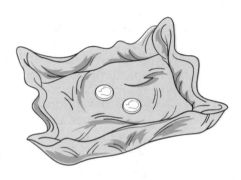

Row, Row, Row Your Boat
(traditional tune)

Row, row, row your boat
Gently down the stream!
Merrily, merrily, merrily, merrily –
Life is but a dream!

Float, float, float your boat
In the water now.
Build a boat that doesn't sink –
Won't you tell me how!

What will "stick" to a magnet?

Building Bridges: Search With Magnets

Hide several metal objects that are attracted to magnets in the sand table or sandbox. Invite the children to find the objects by moving magnets through the sand. Encourage the children to count the number of objects they found!

Note: Magnet wands are great tools to use for this activity.

Predict and Prove

Set out a variety of small objects and a very strong magnet. Encourage the children to sort the items into two groups – those that will stick to a magnet and those that won't. After all the items have been sorted, have the children test their predictions. The children will probably be surprised to find that most, but not all, metal objects will stick to a magnet. Metals containing iron or steel will stick to the magnet.

Note: Be sure to include several metal objects that will be attracted to the magnet (e.g., paper clips), and a few metal objects that will not be attracted to the magnet (e.g., most coins), and some nonmetal objects.

Magnet Magic!

Magnetic force is the push or pull that comes from a magnet. Perform this "magic trick" to explore the pull force of magnets, but don't reveal the secret until the end! You will need two 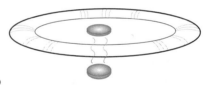 strong magnets and a paper plate. Place one magnet on top of the paper plate, and secretly place the other magnet below the paper plate so the two magnets attract (stick together). Show the audience the magnet on the top of the plate but do not tell them about the magnet on the bottom. Say something like, "I will now use my magic powers to move this magnet around the plate without ever touching it!" Move the hidden magnet around the plate, which in turn will cause the top magnet to move. Now that's some amazing, yet scientific, magic! Of course, provide several opportunities for the children to practice performing this magnet "magic trick" on their own.

Move With Magnets

Use this fun activity to explore the push force of magnets. You will need two strong magnets and a toy car. Securely tape one magnet to the top of the car. Challenge the children to move the car using just the push force of the other magnet. How? Angle the magnet in your hand until the two magnets repel one another. With some practice, you can use the push force to make the car move!

What is static electricity?
How do switches work?

Building Bridges: Electrical Safety

Caution! Danger! Warning! These are all words that the children should think of when you mention electricity. It is very important to reinforce electric safety rules with young children, and what better time than the present! Although rules for children should usually be stated in the positive, such as saying, "walk safely" instead of "don't run," give the children a "Do NOT" list for electric safety to send a very clear and important message. Below are just a few important rules to review with the children:

- Do NOT put anything into an outlet by yourself. Ask an adult for help!
- Do NOT put anything electric near water (like a hair dryer near a sink or bathtub).
- Do NOT swim during a thunderstorm.
- Do NOT touch wires or cables that have fallen down.

Explore Static Electricity

Did you ever have a "bad hair day" when your hair just seems to keep flying away? That's static electricity! Static electricity is also that little shock you get on a cold winter day, or when your socks stick to your sweater when they come out of the dryer. Give each child a small balloon that is already blown up and tied. Invite the children to rub the balloon all over their hair for a few minutes. Have the children hold the balloon near the wall and watch it "stick."

Caution: Always supervise closely when working with balloons. If a balloon should pop, gather all the pieces and discard immediately where the children will not have access to them. Balloon pieces can become a choking hazard if swallowed.

Turn "Switches" On and Off

Turn a light switch on and off a few times. Ask the children to describe what is happening. Explain that when electricity is allowed to flow in a circle, the lights turn on. When the circle is broken, the lights turn off. Turn the light switch on and off again, each time saying "on" and "off." Further explain that all electrical devices with on and off switches (those you plug in and those that use batteries) work the same way. When you turn your radio on, the electricity can flow in a circle and you hear music. When you turn your radio off, the circle is broken.

Invite the children to pretend they are radios. Have the children make a circle with their arms in front of them to "turn on their switches," and put their arms down at their sides to "turn off their switches." When they are on, encourage them to sing and dance. When they are off, encourage them to be silent and stand still. Reinforce the concept by turning on and off the light switch as they pretend.

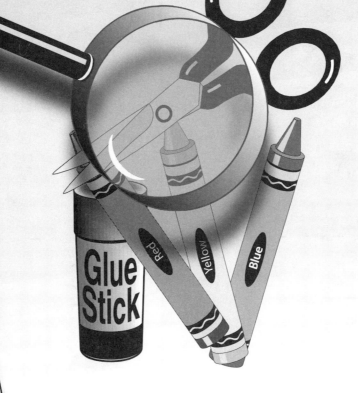

Reproducibles

Life Cycle of a Plant

Super Science

Life Cycle of a Frog

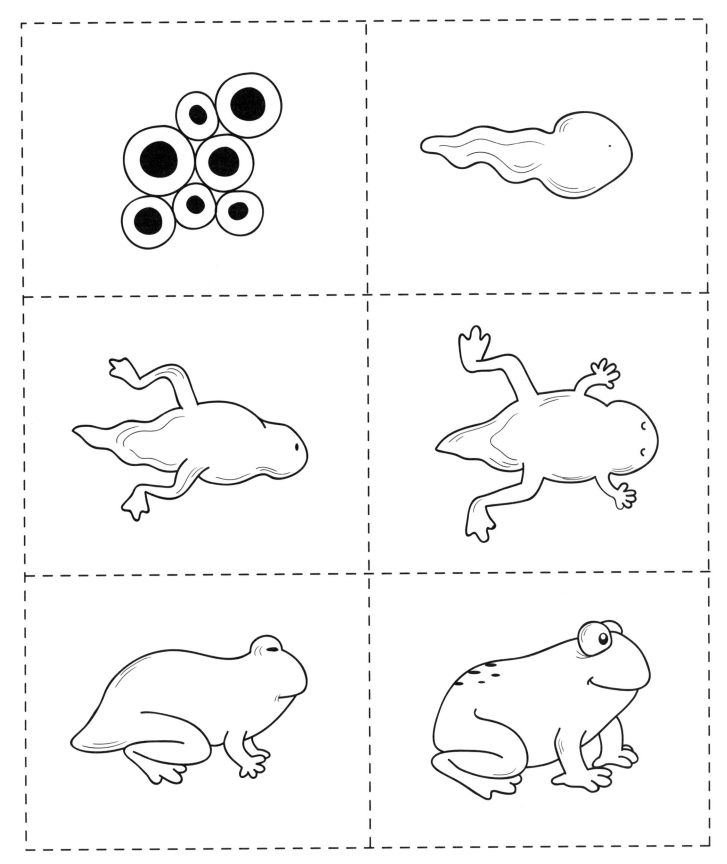

egg

caterpillar

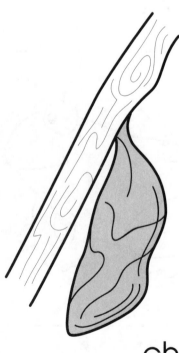

chrysalis

butterfly

Penguin

Animal Babies

DINO BINGO

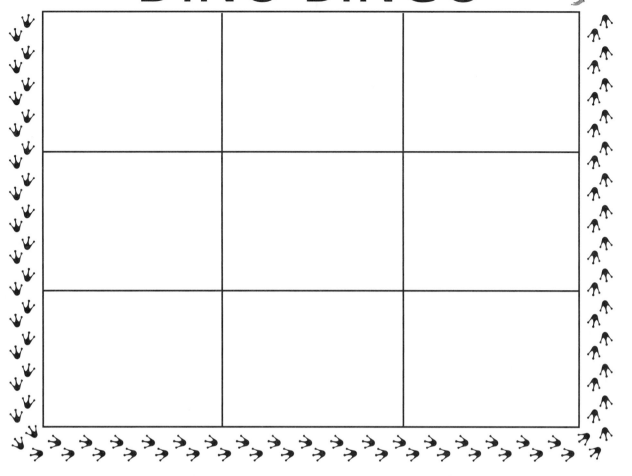

The Water Cycle

Super Science

Super Scientist

Name

Date

Teacher

Signature